BEN LILLY'S TALES
OF
BEARS, LIONS
AND HOUNDS

Ben Lilly as portrayed by Silver City, New Mexico, artist Lois Duffy.

BEN LILLY'S TALES
OF
BEARS, LIONS
AND HOUNDS

Edited by
Neil B. Carmony

High-Lonesome Books

Introduction, afterword, and notes
copyright © 1998 by Neil B. Carmony.

ISBN-13: 978-0-944383-82-7
ISBN-10: 0-944383-82-3
Library of Congress Card #98-73442

Second Printing, 2004
Third Printing, 2010
Fourth Printing, 2016, paperback

High-Lonesome Books
P.O. Box 878
Silver City, New Mexico 88062

DEDICATION

To Fay Bowe and the late Bob Lomax (1911-1996), relatives of Ben Lilly. Their continuing interest in Ben has helped keep the memory of the master houndsman alive.

ACKNOWLEDGEMENTS

The editor wishes to thank Fay Bowe of Mer Rouge, Louisiana; Warren White of Mer Rouge; Delores Lomax of Longview, Texas; Gary Sanders of Tucson, Arizona; Dexter K. Oliver of Tucson; Carolyn O'Bagy Davis of Tucson; Cherie and M. H. "Dutch" Salmon of Silver City, New Mexico; Billy Joe Collyge, of Silver City; Johnny Thompson of Silver City; Cal Salars of Silver City; Norman G. Woolsey of Mesa, Arizona; Leolla Tirey Duncan of Clovis, California; Harley G. Shaw of Chino Valley, Arizona; David E. Brown of Phoenix; and Robert D. Fisher, Collections Manager of Mammals, National Museum of Natural History, Washington, D.C., for their generous assistance. And special thanks to the late J. Frank Dobie for rescuing Ben Lilly's writings from oblivion.

CONTENTS

Editor's Introduction 1
1. Bears and Lions by Ben V. Lilly 14
2. Mountain Lions of New Mexico by Ben V. Lilly 33
3. Bears of Arizona and New Mexico by Ben V. Lilly 59
4. Ben Lilly's Mountain Lion Kill Record for 1916 70
5. Ben Lilly's Idaho Hunting Diary, 1922 86
6. Photographs and Drawings 114
Editor's Afterword: The Ben Lilly Memorials 148
Appendix A: Letters from Ben Lilly to Friends and Colleagues... 153
Appendix B: Letters from Ben Lilly to His Daughters................. 169
Appendix C: Letters Written by Ben Lilly's Children 179
Appendix D: A Newspaper Reporter Interviews Ben Lilly........... 185
Appendix E: Zoological Specimens Collected by Ben Lilly 190
Citations 194
Sources and References 197
Index 207

The famous Taos, New Mexico, artist W. Herbert Dunton painted this portrait of Ben Lilly in 1921. Ben's hunting horn was for calling hounds, not for carrying gunpowder. His rifle is a Winchester Model 1886.

EDITOR'S INTRODUCTION

In 1982 Dale Lee (1908-1988), Arizona's most renowned hunting guide, recorded his recollections of hounds, hunts, and hunters on a series of audio tapes. On one of them he remarked, "I've been asked many times by many different people about who I thought was the greatest hunter that I had ever known or had ever heard of. To me, Ben Lilly was the greatest hunter that ever hit the country out there a'hunting lion and bear." This is a compelling endorsement, coming as it does from Dale Lee, the most experienced mountain lion, black bear, and jaguar hunter of his generation. The Lee family moved from Texas to southeastern Arizona in 1910 when Dale was just a child. Lilly (1856-1936) was in his fifties when he arrived in the region a year later. The two hound men met on the trail a few times in the late 1920s. Dale was just starting out as a professional predator hunter, working primarily in New Mexico, and Ben was near the end of his long career as a killer of cats and bears.

Dale's oldest brother, Ernest Lee (1888-1957), knew Ben Lilly better than Dale did, and he was the source of most of Dale's Lilly lore. Ernest was a bear and lion hunter, and occasionally he would encounter Ben and his dogs deep in a remote canyon or high on the slopes of a wild mountain. Later he told his brothers many campfire stories about Lilly, and the ones that impressed Dale the most focused on Ben's physical stamina. Ben Lilly almost always hunted on foot, only rarely rode a horse or mule. When his hounds were trailing game, he followed them at a shuffling trot, which, no matter how rough the terrain, he could maintain for hours. According to the Lees, at the age of seventy Lilly's ability to run mile after mile after

Ben Lilly's Tales

his baying pack remained undiminished. And even if the tales they related about Lilly's amazing feats of wilderness travel were only partially true, the old hunter would have been a mountain rambler without peer.

Ben Lilly's Early Years

(Unless otherwise indicated, the biographical information in this introduction is taken from Lilly's own writings or from Frank Dobie's book *The Ben Lilly Legend* published in 1950.)

Benjamin Vernon Lilly was born in rural Wilcox County, Alabama, on December 31, 1856. He was the first of what ultimately would be a brood of seven Lilly children. Soon after Ben arrived the family moved to Kemper County, Mississippi, and Ben spent his youth there. His father, Albert Lilly, was a blacksmith and he taught Ben the rudiments of fashioning tools out of steel. Ben's mother, Margaret Ann McKay Lilly, was a teacher. But despite his mother's vocation, Ben hated schoolwork. He left home when in his early teens and after a while joined a bachelor uncle, Vernon Lilly, in northeastern Louisiana. The elder Lilly owned a prosperous farm in Morehouse Parish, near Bonne Idee Bayou. Ben eventually inherited the property, but the wild canebrakes and swamps, not the cotton fields, were where Ben spent most of his time.

In the fall of 1880, at the age of twenty-three, Ben married Lelia Bunckley despite being warned that she was a little "tetched in the head." In due course a child was born, a son Ben and Lelia named Vernon. But the sickly boy died when very young, and after his death his parents divorced. Lelia was eventually committed to an insane asylum. Ben fared better and began to earn a reputation as an expert hunter. But between hunts Ben found time to court and win another bride. On February 9, 1891, he exchanged marriage vows with Mary Etta Sisson (1867-1931). They made their home on the outskirts of the town of Mer Rouge, Louisiana. During the next seven years their union produced three children, a boy named Hugh (1891-1918) and two girls, Ada Mai (1893-1969) and Beatrice Verna (1897-1985).[1]

Ben disliked farming and made a living for Mary and the children first by trading in cattle and then by cutting and selling timber. And he spent more and more time hunting. Often he would be gone from home for weeks, hunting deer and waterfowl for the market, alligators for their hides, black bears for their meat and grease, and panthers (as mountain lions are known in the South) simply because they needed killing. Ben believed that God had placed him on earth specifically to hunt, and he zealously strove to fulfill his bloody assignment. Bears and panthers, killers of livestock, were then considered vermin by everyone, not just by God and Ben, and Lilly and his dogs took after them with remorseless fury.

Naturally, Ben's long absences from his family took its toll on his marriage. In 1901 he transferred all his property to his wife, kissed his children good-bye, and disappeared into the forest. From then on hunting was his sole occupation and a simple camp deep in the woods his only home. At the age of forty-four Ben Lilly rejected the twentieth century and adopted the lonely, nomadic life of a "mountain man" in the tradition of Old Bill Williams.

In 1904 a chance meeting with Ned Hollister (1876-1924), a naturalist employed by the Bureau of Biological Survey (forerunner of the U.S. Fish and Wildlife Service), resulted in Ben Lilly acquiring a rewarding sideline. Hollister was in Louisiana collecting wildlife specimens for scientific study when Lilly came to his attention as an authority on the local game animals. Ned liked Ben and recruited him to collect mammals and birds for the U.S. National Museum, a part of the Smithsonian Institution in Washington. The young naturalist trained Lilly in the techniques of preparing skins and skulls, and over the years Ben sold many specimens to the museum (see Appendix E).

In 1906 Ben Lilly shifted his base of operations to the Big Thicket of East Texas. Louisiana had ceased to be a bear and panther hunter's paradise, and, although there was more game in the Big Thicket, it, too, was under siege as a wilderness. In December 1906 Lilly participated in one of the last notable bear hunts to take place in the region. Organized by Hardin County hound men Ben and Bud Hooks (the Hooks brothers were hunting legends in their own right), the expedition included a large crowd of their friends and guests. Two of the hunters were from Topeka, Kansas: L. L. Kiene, a feature writer for the *Topeka State Journal*, and John

Strickrott, a prominent photographer. Ben Lilly killed one of the two bears taken during the chase, the other was killed by writer Kiene. In his article describing the adventure, Kiene stated that the bear he bagged was his first and Ben's was his 118th. Kiene went on to note that the Big Thicket was shrinking fast as loggers cut the forests and farmers plowed the cleared land. Bears and the men who hunted them would soon be rare species in East Texas. Three of John Strickrott's photos are reproduced in Chapter 6.

Teddy Roosevelt and the Ben Lilly Legend

In October 1907 President Theodore Roosevelt (1858-1919), accompanied by a number of other dignitaries, went on a two-week hunt in the nearly-impenetrable thickets of northeastern Louisiana. Teddy's hosts were New Orleans businessman John M. Parker (who would later serve as governor of Louisiana) and Avery Island planter and former Rough Rider John A. McIlhenny. The president's primary object was to bag a black bear "after the fashion of the old southern planters, who for a century past have followed the bear with horse and hound and horn." But bears were no longer abundant in the region and it looked like he might have to return to Washington empty handed. The hunters moved their camp from Tensas Bayou to Bear Lake, twenty miles to the south, but their quarry remained elusive. At last, after twelve days of fruitless trailing, the dogs owned by guides Clive and Harley Metcalfe jumped a good-sized bear and Roosevelt shot it.

Ben Lilly was one of several hound men summoned from near and far to find game for the nation's most famous sportsman. The setting for the presidential hunt was in country Ben knew like the back of his hand, so he was a logical choice to participate in the affair. When word reached him that his services were needed, Ben immediately set out for Tensas Bayou. While some writers have stated that Lilly was "chief huntsman" for the expedition, Roosevelt made no such assertion and credited the Metcalfes and their dog handler, Holt Collier (a former slave), with being the men "to whom we owed the success of our hunt." Nevertheless, Teddy was impressed by Lilly, and he discussed the backwoodsman in a letter he wrote to his sixteen-year-old daughter, Ethel:

Introduction

Camp on Tensas Bayou,
Oct. 6, 1907.

Darling Ethel:
    Here we are in camp. It is very picturesque, and as comfortable as possible. We have a big fly tent for the horses; the hounds sleep with them, or with the donkeys! There is a white hunter, Ben Lilly, who has just joined us, who is really a remarkable character. He literally lives in the woods. He joined us early this morning, with one dog. He had tramped for twenty-four hours through the woods, without food or water, and had slept a couple of hours in a crooked tree, like a wild turkey.
    He has a mild, gentle face, blue eyes, and full beard; he is a religious fanatic, and is as hardy as a bear or elk, literally caring nothing for fatigue and exposure, which we couldn't stand at all. He doesn't seem to consider the 24 hours' trip he has just made, any more than I should a half hour's walk before breakfast. He quotes the preacher Talmage continually . . . .[2]

Thomas DeWitt Talmage (1832-1902), Ben Lilly's spiritual mentor, was one of the best-known clergymen of his day. He was trained at the Dutch Reformed seminary in New Brunswick, New Jersey, but later joined the Presbyterians. Talmage wrote many books, mostly diatribes exhorting the faithful to turn their backs on Demon Rum, loose women, Mormonism, and other evils. His sermons were published in newspapers throughout the country, and Talmage contributed hundreds of articles to pious magazines. The theatrics and bizarre gestures he employed while preaching enthralled his followers, were ridiculed by his critics. In 1879 Presbyterian officials charged Talmage with "using improper methods of preaching, which tend to bring religion into contempt." A church panel acquitted him, but the vote was close.[3]

    In accordance with his religious convictions, derived in part from Talmage's teachings, Ben Lilly abstained from strong drink, never took the Lord's name in vain or used coarse language of any kind, avoided illicit liaisons with women, and did absolutely nothing on Sunday but rest and read the Bible. His rule against performing even the smallest task on the Sabbath was rarely breached. Although Lilly was rigid in his beliefs, he was not overbearing and never attempted to convert others to his way of thinking. After he left his family he rarely if ever attended church services, and he didn't claim membership in any particular Christian denomination. Like the other aspects of his later life, Lilly's religious regimen was distinctly his own.

Roosevelt described Ben Lilly in more detail in a story he wrote about the bear hunt for *Scribner's Magazine*. Titled "In the Louisiana Canebrakes," the article was published in the January 1908 issue. His comments about Lilly were these:

> The morning after we reached camp we were joined by Ben Lilly, the hunter, a spare, full-bearded man, with wild, gentle, blue eyes and a frame of steel and whipcord. I never met any other man so indifferent to fatigue and hardship. He equalled Cooper's Deerslayer in woodcraft, in hardihood, in simplicity—and also in loquacity. The morning he joined us in camp, he had come on foot through the thick woods, followed by his two dogs, and had neither eaten nor drunk for twenty-four hours; for he did not like to drink the swamp water. It had rained hard throughout the night and he had no shelter, no rubber coat, nothing but the clothes he was wearing, and the ground was too wet for him to lie on; so he perched in a crooked tree in the beating rain, much as if he had been a wild turkey. But he was not in the least tired when he struck camp; and, though he slept an hour after breakfast, it was chiefly because he had nothing else to do, inasmuch as it was Sunday, on which day he never hunted nor labored. He could run through the woods like a buck, was far more enduring, and quite as indifferent to weather, though he was over fifty years old. He had trapped

and hunted throughout almost all the half century of his life, and on trail of game he was as sure as his own hounds. His observations on wild creatures were singularly close and accurate. He was particularly fond of the chase of the bear, which he followed by himself, with one or two dogs; often he would be on the trail of his quarry for days at a time, lying down to sleep wherever night overtook him; and he had killed over a hundred and twenty bears.

Here we have the core of the Ben Lilly "legend" presented to the reading public by none other than the president of the United States. Roosevelt's brief remarks set the tone for descriptions of the houndsman for years to come.

Ben Lilly Leaves the South

A few months after his hunt with Teddy Roosevelt, Ben Lilly left the swampy South, now nearly devoid of panthers and bears. In July 1908 Ben and his faithful hounds crossed the Rio Grande at Eagle Pass, Texas, and headed into Mexico where game was more plentiful. Northern Coahuila was his first Mexican hunting ground, and there he made ends meet by collecting specimens for the National Museum and by supplying mining camps with venison. He migrated west in 1910 and entered the state of Chihuahua. A few grizzlies could still be found in Chihuahua, and Lilly (or possibly a sportsman he guided) bagged one of the majestic bears. In November 1910 Lilly shipped the skull of this grizzly, an adult male, to Washington from Gallego, a railroad station about eighty miles north of Chihuahua City. According to museum records, the bear was killed eleven miles west of Gallego.[4] Mammalogists, especially Dr. C. Hart Merriam (1855-1942) who was conducting an exhaustive taxonomic study of grizzlies, were eager to obtain as many grizzly specimens as possible, and the National Museum paid good money for them. Chapter 6 includes a photo of Lilly with the Gallego bear.

Lilly's stay in Chihuahua was brief. The Mexican Revolution erupted in fall of 1910, and early in 1911 Ben prudently crossed the border into New Mexico. There and in adjacent Arizona he made a living hunting stock-killing predators for the bounties offered by ranchers. He plied his trade from New Mexico's Boot Heel north to Arizona's White Mountains and Blue River watershed. Mountain lions and black bears were Lilly's bread and butter, but he and his dogs managed to locate and conquer one of the last grizzlies to inhabit the region—its skull is in the National Museum. The bear was killed in 1913 on the east slopes of the White Mountains. The museum houses another grizzly skull from Arizona sent in by Lilly. This one, collected "near Blue," arrived in Washington in 1915. It is weathered and undoubtedly a skull that Lilly found along the trail. Because of their monetary value as specimens, it is unlikely that Lilly discarded any grizzly skulls that came into his possession.[5]

On March 4, 1915, the U.S. Congress enacted legislation creating a federal program designed to rid the national forests and public domain lands of wild animals deemed a menace to the livestock industry. The Bureau of Biological Survey was given an initial appropriation of $125,000 to begin this endeavor.[6] For decades thereafter, Congress provided money each year to continue the war on "noxious" animals found on the Western ranges.

When the Biological Survey began to organize its predator-control program and hire field men to carry it out, Ben Lilly was already known to Survey officials in Washington, such as Dr. Albert K. Fisher (1856-1948), through the specimens he had collected for them. At the suggestion of Dr. Fisher, in 1916 J. Stokley Ligon (1879-1961), head of the Biological Survey's predator eradication efforts in Arizona and New Mexico, hired Lilly to hunt mountain lions and bears for the government.[7] Ben was fifty-nine years old and must have been the oldest man on Ligon's staff. His hunting territory included the mountains and canyons of southwestern New Mexico and southeastern Arizona. (All of Lilly's Arizona hunts took place in Greenlee County.)

Ben Lilly and his hounds caught large predators for the Biological Survey intermittently from 1916 to 1920. During these years the government paid him for about thirty months of work, and Survey records show that he accounted for fifty-five lions, twelve bears, two bobcats, and one coyote.[8] But Ben was unsuited for government employment and the regimentation it entailed. To the dismay of his bosses, he paid no attention to game regulations and shot deer out of season when he needed them to feed himself or his dogs. Finally, Ben's supervisors came to the conclusion that he was spending too much time looking for bears and was neglecting mountain lions, which they judged the greater threat to livestock. In August 1920 his "services were terminated."[9] Upon his dismissal from the Survey, Ben took a vacation of sorts and visited his brother Joe in Mineral Wells, Texas, and his sister Margaret Mills in Shreveport, Louisiana.[10] He then went back to his Southwest hunting grounds.

For most of 1921 and 1922 Lilly was on the payroll of William H. McFadden (1869-1956), a wealthy Oklahoma oil executive and avid sportsman. For nearly two years Lilly and several other hound men guided McFadden and his companions in their quest for grizzlies (none were killed), black bears, mountain lions, and other trophies. This amazing hunt was and is unparalleled in its scope and duration. It began in southwestern New Mexico in the spring of 1921 and moved north in stages in search of ever-richer game fields. The hunting party finally disbanded in Idaho in the fall of 1922.

Upon returning to New Mexico, Lilly was hired by the foreman of the large G.O.S. Ranch to make the outfit's pastures safe for cows. The G.O.S. was situated in the Gila National Forest north of Silver City, and it encompassed some of the best lion and bear country in the Southwest. Ben became a fixture at the ranch, and it was during this period that the peculiar but genial old woodsman became firmly established as a New Mexico folk personality.[11] Of course, by today's standards Ben Lilly was an insensitive destroyer of wildlife. But at the time he lived, the men who were paid to exterminate mountain lions, grizzly bears, and other stock-killing "varmints" were viewed as good citizens performing necessary work.

As the decade of the '20s drew to a close Ben spent less time hunting and more time making knives, painting pictures of the animals he had hunted for so many years, and making and decorating hunting horns. His knives were sturdy and well proportioned, just the kind of tools a "mountain man" would appreciate. Ben's paintings and sketches had a simple, stylized quality reminiscent of Indian rock art. He didn't sell his works, rather he gave them to friends and relatives.

In 1932 Ben moved from the G.O.S. (which had new owners) to Tom O'Brien's ranch in the Mimbres Valley a few miles to the south. But Ben's mind had begun to fail, and soon he was no longer able to care for himself. In the spring of 1933 Grant County officials took him to the county "poor farm" located about fifty miles northwest of Silver City. Ben died there on December 17, 1936, at the age of seventy-nine. His funeral and burial were at Silver City, and his daughters came from Texas and Louisiana to say good-bye a second and final time. Hugh Lilly was not present because he had preceded his father in death. He passed away in 1918 at the age of twenty-six, a victim of tuberculosis. Ben Lilly had no grandchildren to mourn his passing.[12]

J. Frank Dobie Meets Ben Lilly

In January 1928 Texas folklorist and writer Frank Dobie (1888-1964) ran into Ben Lilly in El Paso. Lilly had come to town with Victor Culberson, manager and part owner of the G.O.S. Ranch, to talk to a meeting of the American National Livestock Association about predatory animals. This would be Lilly's first and only foray into formal public speaking, and it must have been quite an event. In the course of their El Paso encounter Lilly showed Dobie two typed manuscripts, one about mountain lions, the other about bears. Dobie read them with great interest and made a mental note that he would try to learn more about his new friend when time permitted. But the two never met again.

Frank Dobie didn't forget about Ben Lilly and in the summer of 1940 began a search for his manuscripts and other papers. He never located the typescripts he had seen in El Paso but did find two handwritten copies of Lilly's discourse on lions. One was in the possession of Harvey Forsythe of Santa Rita, New Mexico. The other lion manuscript, virtually identical to the first one, had been left by Lilly with L. A. Jessen, a Bayard, New Mexico, dentist. Both were written in pencil on cheap tablet paper. Forsythe also had Lilly's record of mountain lions killed from June to September 1916 and a portion of a bear story. But the pages of the bear manuscript were badly damaged and only partially readable. At that time Dobie was on the faculty of the University of Texas at Austin, and he had his secretary make verbatim typescripts of these documents.

Fortunately, an article on bears and lions written by Lilly had found its way into print. It appeared in the July and August 1928 issues of *The Producer*, the official magazine of the American National Livestock Association. Dobie eventually acquired a typed copy of a diary kept by Lilly covering the period May to October 1922. The original had been sent by Lilly to William McFadden. The diary chronicled the Idaho portion of the elaborate two-year hunting campaign sponsored by the oil tycoon.

During the next decade Frank Dobie searched far and wide for people who had known Ben Lilly. As it turned out, just about everyone who had met Ben remembered him and had a story or two to tell about his remarkable exploits. (For reasons of their own, Ben's daughters did not respond to Dobie's inquiries.) Ben Lilly was absolutely unique and thus unforgettable. But to say that people admired him would not be accurate—he was too odd for that. The old hunter with untrimmed beard and scruffy clothes was not really the sort of man they wanted their sons to emulate. After leaving the South, Ben's increasingly strange ways, such as his reluctance to sleep indoors or even to enter a house, precluded his having close friends. But regardless of his eccentricities, Ben was friendly, polite, cheerful, rather dignified in bearing, and, all-in-all, very likeable. Out of fond respect for the old mountaineer, in 1947 a group of his acquaintances placed a bronze plaque bearing his likeness on a slab of granite in the forest a few miles north of Silver City. Fifty years later the Mer Rouge, Louisiana, Lions Club, inspired by hunter and Lilly fan Warren White, erected a monument honoring Ben in front of the local post office. These memorials are discussed further in the "Editor's Afterword."

Dobie's research resulted in the book *The Ben Lilly Legend*. First published in 1950, the work has gone through several editions and is still in print. It has boosted Ben Lilly from an obscure local curiosity to a folk hero known throughout the country. Few hunters have been fortunate enough to have writers of Dobie's skill for their biographers.

The title of Dobie's book was well chosen—among the people who had known him, Ben Lilly had become a legendary figure.

According to Dobie's informants, Ben could run faster, jump higher, and shoot straighter than any man of his day. Although not a large man (about 5' 9" tall), he was amazingly strong and on several occasions engaged in hand-to-hand combat with bears, slaying the enraged beasts with his homemade hunting knife. Ben's sense of direction was unerring, and his tracking ability astonished even the most seasoned woodsmen. His skill with a rifle was so well-honed he could shoot the bill off a flying duck. Sherlock Holmes had nothing on Ben Lilly. From a single print made by a bear's paw the master hunter could tell with precise accuracy when the track was made, the age, sex, and weight of the animal, where the bear had been, where it was going, why it was going there, and when it would return. And, like George Washington, Ben Lilly never told a lie.

A good deal of this was folklore, of course. Regardless of how capable Lilly actually was, there was always room for storytellers to enlarge on the truth for the benefit of listeners. Contrary to what one would expect of a reclusive backwoodsman, Lilly was talkative when he had an audience and loved to tell people about his adventures. How many of the exaggerated yarns regarding his prowess can be attributed to the garrulous hunter himself is hard to determine, but Ben was not above overstating the facts. In a letter written in 1943, Dr. A. K. Fisher, who hunted with Lilly in New Mexico's Black Range in 1918, recalled that he found Ben to be truthful in most matters, but "when he was with a crowd telling stories, he often shot with the long bow." An example of Ben's tendency to magnify his abilities appears in a 1928 letter he wrote to an old friend in Louisiana: "I am sure I improve in shooting all the time. If a bear or lion ever jumps out of a tree and I am in sight, I will get three balls in it before it hits the ground."

The Writings Presented in This Book

Shortly before his death in 1988, hound man Dale Lee gave many of his personal effects to his friend and fellow Tucson resident Gary Sanders. In the summer of 1997 Gary generously allowed me to examine the documents that had belonged to Dale. In a large box filled mostly with old letters were copies of Ben Lilly's mountain lion and bear manuscripts, Lilly's record of mountain lion kills for

1916, and his 1922 Idaho diary. These are published for the first time in this volume, along with the article that appeared in *The Producer* in 1928. Several of Ben's letters are included as appendices. These works constitute the known writings of Ben Lilly, save other letters unavailable to the editor. Needless to say, reading Lilly's own words is the best way to get a glimpse into his world of hounds, bears, and lions. Did Ben Lilly live up to the legend so masterfully presented by Frank Dobie? We will let the reader decide.

1

BEARS AND LIONS

By Ben V. Lilly

Editor's note: In January 1928 Ben Lilly, now seventy-one years old, gave a talk about predatory animals at a convention in El Paso sponsored by the American National Livestock Association. After his presentation, representatives of *The Producer*, the official journal of the Association, asked Lilly to write an article recounting his experiences as a hunter of mountain lions and bears. Ben complied with their request. His autobiographical narrative appeared in the July and August 1928 issues of *The Producer*, and it is reprinted here. The staff of the magazine undoubtedly corrected Lilly's grammar and spelling, but they do not appear to have been heavy-handed in their editing.

Besides providing explanatory notes in brackets, this editor has felt compelled to point out those instances where Lilly's ideas regarding bear and lion biology and behavior conflict with the findings of modern research. For example, Lilly consistently overstates the amount of social interaction that occurs in the wild between adult mountain lions. He does the same with bears. Researchers have found that, except for mating, the adults of both groups are much more solitary in their habits than Lilly believed them to be. Keep in mind that Ben's direct observations of these animals were limited to how they reacted to dogs and bullets. Ben attempted to kill each and every lion and bear he encountered and never spent time merely watching them.

◇ ◇ ◇ ◇ ◇

This article is intended to describe the destructiveness of bears and mountain lions on stock ranches. I will take up my hunts as they come to mind and relate things as I remember them.

I will begin by going back to March 9, 1910 [*1911*], when I was in my camp at the head of the Animas Mountains [*in the southwestern corner of New Mexico*]. I started out that morning at about nine o'clock. I found the tracks of two lions—a full-grown female and a half-grown animal. The tracks seemed to be about a week old. I had no hounds, but an Airedale dog. I also found the track of a full-grown brown bear. I could tell that he was brown because I found brown hair on a bush that he had rubbed on. I worked on the track until dark. That night I went to my camp.

[*There were two species of bears in the region, black bears and grizzlies. Many "black" bears are, of course, quite black, but, in the Southwest, various shades of brown, from dark chocolate to light tan or blonde, occur among them.[13] The grizzlies also varied in color, and individuals exhibited sundry shades of brown, with lighter, often grayish, guard hairs.[14]*]

Next morning I was out at daylight. I soon tracked the bear up. He was eating off the head of a sotol [*desert spoon*]. Sotol is a vegetable, and at time bears eat them. This fellow had eaten two or three heads and had gone into a thick brush—so dense that it was impossible to see a bear even at a distance of twenty steps. I soon found the bed where he lay that night, but he was gone. I followed his track all day, keeping a close watch for him. The Airedale dog asked to be excused when he smelled the bear's bed. He stayed away behind me—no bear track for him! I tracked that bear until dark, when I built a fire and lay down for the night.

That night the bear had gone down a branch of the river [*Animas Creek?*] for a long distance, wading in the water. I finally found where he had come out and made a bed and lain down in it. Then he struck out for another day's travel. He went to another big hole that he had scratched in the ground, bit down bushes, and covered over the hole with the brush. He seemed to have stayed in that place for over a week [?], but went on when he found me tracking him. He went by where he had killed a two-year-old steer. It seemed that he had had quite a tussle to kill the steer. The small bushes bore evidence that he had wallowed [*fought?*] the steer more than usual

Ben Lilly's Tales

for a bear, as they generally kill cattle right on the spot. Two of his toes were off on one front foot, which showed very plainly on the tracks he made. He never ate one mouthful of the steer but struck out for Old Mexico. I followed him until I found he had crossed the line, when I came back and waited a couple of weeks.

While waiting, I went out to buy a couple of burros. I had a young man keeping camp for me. I sent him to a neighbor's house for something. He carried my gun with him and forgot to bring the ammunition back to camp. [*Ben's favorite rifle for dispatching Southwest bears was reportedly a Winchester Model 1886 in .33 W.C.F. caliber.*] So I took an empty shotgun along, thinking I might trade it for burros. The man I went to see did not want to sell. In coming back to camp, I made a search for lion tracks. I had a young, unbroken hound dog with me. He seemed fond of running rabbits, so I let him chase rabbits. The first thing I noticed, he was running down a hill as fast as he could go and making a growling noise. I ran over to see what he was after and found that there was a full-grown female lion running him.

When I saw the lion, she was humped up and standing still. I tried to run up on the lion and hit her with the empty gun. She broke away, with me and the dog after her. She ran up a tree, jumped out, and ran up another tree. I chunked her with rocks. She treed again. I chunked her out. She ran up another tree. I chunked her out the fifth time [?]. The rock I threw at her struck her in the mouth. I noticed she was a little stunned. It was a very low tree. I sprang up in the tree and grabbed her by the tail and jumped out, holding her tail in my hand. We hit the ground all in a bundle together.

The lion struck out, running down grade, with me gaining on her. I had a fairly good stick in my hand. It was a green pine stick. I struck her on the back as she was passing around the top of a small pine log that fell down on the ground. She sprang at me. I struck her over the head with the pine stick and broke the stick in two. She kept coming. I broke the stick five times [?] over her head. She came so fast that I grabbed up a large rock that would weigh about six pounds and held it tight in my hand. I pounded her on the side of her head, and she fell at my feet, apparently dead. I had a small knife in my pocket, with a blade two and a quarter inches long. I tried to stick this into her heart. I felt I had succeeded in doing so. She seemed to be dead.

I sat down, and the dog came up. I wanted him to bite her a little. The dog was afraid to come up when I was chunking her, and he did not come near at any time while I was fighting. So I made him bite her. I thought it would do the dog some good. He took two or three bites on her hind legs. Up she came and made for me. I grabbed up a big rock and gave the same kind of a blow on the side of her head as she grabbed at me and downed her. I pounded her on the head until I felt the skull was crushed. I then reached her heart with the little knife. She measured six feet eight inches long—a full-grown female mountain lion. I had no ammunition and had a hand-to-hand fight.

In two or three days I went down to the United States soldiers' camp at the border of Old Mexico. I told the man in charge of the soldiers that I wanted to go over on the Mexican side to hunt up a big brown bear that I had been trailing on the Diamond A Ranch several days before. [*The ranch where Lilly ran into this bear was founded in 1881 by Michael Gray, then sold in 1883 and incorporated into the "Diamond A" operation. The property, now again known as the "Gray Ranch," is presently owned by the Animas Foundation.*[15]] He said he would send two or three men over with me. So I went down, and the man and myself struck out. I found the bear's tracks, and I was anxious to find a good place to trap him. About two o'clock that afternoon the man said to me: "I've got all of the bear-hunting I want. Let's go [*back*] to camp" [*in the U.S.*]. [*I said:*] "You go, and I will find a good place to catch that bear before I leave these mountains." Then he said good-bye. About three days later I went to their camp [*the U.S. Army camp across the line*] and told them I had two bears hanging up in the mountains, and if they would give me three or four men and horses, we would go and bring the bear meat out. We brought out two bears that night. [*Lilly bagged these bears in the Sierra San Luis, a range of mountains situated on the Continental Divide at the point where New Mexico, Chihuahua, and Sonora converge.*]

The next time I went down [*to Mexico*] I killed a female lion, and I trapped the big brown bear with two toes off his front foot. He had traveled over a rough country, dragging the trap over rocks. He had worn the chain and clog off the trap. I took his track and followed him for several days, killing him late Saturday evening. He was started on Diamond A Ranch on March 9 [*1911*], trailed for three days in the United States, and then went into Old Mexico. I killed him making his way back to the Animas Mountains. I chased him in three states [*New Mexico, Sonora, and Chihuahua*]. His front tusks were worn to the gums, both above and below. That was why he had trouble killing cattle. He was the oldest bear I ever killed.

I killed the largest black female bear that I ever saw and the oldest one. The four large tusks that are usually called the "holders" were worn off the same as on the large brown male bear. The front teeth in both the upper and the lower jaws were worn off down to the bone. The female was killed thirty miles south of the Animas Mountains in the State of Chihuahua, Mexico. I sent the hides and skulls of these two bears to the United States Museum at Washington, D.C., with the data attached to each one. The male was not extra large for that species. The female was larger than any black bear I have found in any locality. I killed eleven mountain lions and thirteen bears [*in New Mexico's Boot Heel and adjacent Old Mexico in 1911*]. The bears were all large and of four varieties—grizzly, big red (the color of a sorrel horse), black, and brown. I also killed some large wolves.

[*Because Lilly and other old-timers often referred to grizzlies as simply "big bears," and because in the 1850s and again in the 1890s boundary surveyors reported encountering grizzlies in the Sierra San Luis, many writers have assumed that the "big brown bear" Ben said he pursued through three states and finally killed near the Chihuahua/New Mexico border was a grizzly.[16] Since Lilly stated he sent the bear's skin and skull to Washington, these should be available for examination. But a search of the U.S. National Museum failed to disclose a grizzly specimen that fits this bear as to locale and year of collection. However, in 1911 Lilly sent the museum five black bear specimens collected in the Sierra San Luis. One of them (USNM No. 177661, skull and skin, sex not indicated) was obtained in the Chihuahua portion of the mountains on May 13, 1911, "twelve miles south of the U.S. line." The hair is orange-brown, and two toes are missing from the right front foot. The teeth* are badly worn indicating a very old animal. This must be Ben's "three-state" bear.[17] Some authors have repeated as fact a story about how Lilly and his pack trailed the three-state "grizzly" continuously for two months and traversed some five hundred miles before killing it north of Silver City. Lilly's firsthand account shows that this is a tall tale.[18]]

I spent three years in Old Mexico [*1908-1911*]. I did well in every section where I hunted and was treated nicely in every locality I have ever worked in. In the latter part of July 1908 I crossed the river [*the Rio Grande*] at Eagle Pass, Texas, and went to a mining town called Mouskiss [*Múzquiz, Coahuila*]. From there I went up to a ranch called La Palma. [*This is probably the San José de la Palma Ranch, located about fifteen miles west of Múzquiz. The ranch is in the foothills of the Sierra Santa Rosa. Another possibility is a site called La Palma about seventy miles northwest of Múzquiz.*] I killed several very fine bears and mountain lions there and had a real good hunt. I hunted north up to Para Blanco Ranch. [*This is the Piedra Blanca Ranch, located about 140 miles northwest of Múzquiz. The ranch is on the east side of the Sierra del Carmen (see Appendix E).*] There I found bears, deer, lions, and turkeys. That was my headquarters. From there I hunted north and east to the Rio Grande River. I killed some very fine black bears, turkeys, two kinds of deer—black-tail and white-tail—antelopes, and javelinas or peccaries. North of the city of Chihuahua there are some of the largest wild turkeys I ever saw. They are said to be the largest species of wild turkey in the world. I know of several ranges where they can be found. I killed several of them when I was in that section. [*It appears that during the short time Ben spent in Chihuahua he did not hunt in the Sierra Madre proper. The few specimens he collected in the state were from outlying mountains (see Appendix E).*]

Old Mexico has wonderful hunting localities. It is such a large country that a man has to be an expert to know how to make a successful hunt in the first place. He would have to look up the feeding-grounds and watering-places of the game. The game may be plentiful one season and scarce the next. The way to overcome these troubles is to do like the wild game—travel over the locality and see where the food and water will be good enough to attract wild game and find out if there has been any game raised in the locality that season. Year-olds do not run away as badly as older ones.

In 1912 I moved from the Animas Mountains to Clifton, Arizona. I heard that there were some grizzlies along the head reaches of the Blue and Frisco [*San Francisco*] rivers [*north of Clifton*]. I went up the Blue River till I came to a man's house. There I camped that night. He told me [*where*] I might find some bears and lions. He rode up that way a few miles with me. I found two lion tracks as I was traveling along. He directed me the way to go to find water and a camping place. I had five burros and five hounds with me. I saw seven places where calves had been killed by lions—say, in about five weeks' time—and saw three different-sized lions' tracks but nothing fresh enough to let the dogs go on.

I camped on what was called the Little Blue [*a creek*] the next day. Some cowboys came by my camp. I asked them if there were any grizzly bears in that section. They said that some bears came through once in a while and that the lions were catching calves and colts. I told them I was after a big male grizzly bear for the museum at Washington and that I had heard there were some on the Blue Range [*Blue River watershed*]. I told them I would look around and see if there was a big one in that section. They said there were some big bears and that they were killing cattle on the ranges. I asked them if they would pay bounty on bears and lions. They said there were three men who would pay some bounty—about five dollars each for lions.

I made a good big search for grizzlies and found bear tracks but no grizzlies. I found four lion tracks and six bear tracks. I sent a man out to see if they would make up a bounty. They failed to organize. I hunted that week, killing six bears and four lions. I carried the hides down to Clifton, but they would pay no bounty as I was by myself when I killed them and the law said I would have to have a witness. I thought I could not find a man who could act as a witness as I hunted afoot and he could not be there when the lion was killed. The men got together and arranged with me to kill the lions and bears for them. The police jury met and took the bounty off the bear hides to keep me from killing them out. The bounty on a bear and lion hide was ten dollars each. So a few men gathered up and started me on the lions and bears. This was the Fourth of July, 1912.

[*By 1912 sentiment was changing in the Southwest regarding bears. Sportsmen wanted them managed as big game with closed seasons and bag limits, arguing that only proven stock killers should be removed by men such as Ben Lilly. New Mexico afforded bears partial protection as game animals in 1927, and in 1929 Arizona did likewise. As a result, healthy populations of black bears continue to thrive in suitable habitats in both states. Regretfully, legal protection came too late to save the grizzly. The Southwest's largest carnivore, already long gone from West Texas, became extinct in both Arizona and New Mexico in the 1930s. The best evidence indicates that the last Mexican grizzlies were killed in Chihuahua in the 1960s, completing the extirpation of the southern populations of the great bear.[19]*]

The lions killed cattle of all sizes. I saw seven calves and yearlings, mixed, killed on the Little Blue that looked as if they were killed inside of five weeks, eaten on by lions and covered up. When I was trailing the four lions I killed and carried their hides to Clifton, I found one full-grown cow killed, one three-year-old heifer, and four calves. They had been killed inside of four weeks. Some of them were freshly eaten on and were covered up with leaves and straw. The six bears had three grown cows they had been eating on. Some had been killed two weeks, and one was fresh. I could find carcasses and old bones in nearly every canyon. Bones of animals that were killed one or two years ago would show, when they were left on rocks or in dry places. Old stock's bones last longer than those of young stock. The mountain lion raises two sets of kittens inside of twelve or fifteen months. They make a number of kills that are never found. They kill in a rough place and hide their kill by dragging it to a thick place and covering it up well.

[*Biologists state that female mountain lions may "have" two litters within fifteen months but cannot "raise" two litters of young in twelve to fifteen months. This simply isn't enough time for two sets of kittens to mature. Research has disclosed that it usually takes from three to four years for female mountain lions to raise two litters. On average, females breed about once every eighteen to twenty-four months. (They may breed more frequently if they lose their litters.) The gestation period for mountain lions is three months, and kittens normally stay with their mother for at least twelve months, often longer. Young "subadult" lions do not remain in contact with their mother after she gives birth to another litter. At that time they must go off and fend for themselves, if they have not already done so.[20]*]

When I came back from Clifton, I was ready to go after a big bear for the museum. I killed forty-seven lions and bears on that range that season, and they [*the ranchers*] commenced to [*successfully*] raise colts.

In the spring of 1913 I hunted on the ranges of the people who were paying me a bounty on bears and lions. That year I killed forty-eight bears and lions—about the same number of each. The snow stayed on late, and the bears killed a great many cattle. On the third day of April I killed the largest grizzly bear I ever bagged. He measured nine feet from the end of his nose to the end of his tail, eight feet around his body, and four feet eight inches in height. His hind foot was twelve inches long and seven inches wide. His front nails were five inches long, measuring from the top side. The skull measured eighteen inches in length. His ankles measured fourteen inches around, both rear and front. The back of his claws at the top of the nail was a broad as a man's finger. The hide [*skull*] is in the museum at Washington and [*the hide*] belongs to me. I want one thousand dollars for it.

I followed him three days in the snow, which was waist-deep to as shallow as knee-deep. I never had one mouthful to eat and had on only a common pair of blue cotton pants, a blue shirt, and a light cotton sweater. I built fires and sat up all night and kept from freezing. I wounded him several times at very long range running from me. He finally charged me from a dense jungle of spruce and got within fifteen feet of me before I saw him. He was only three feet away when I shot him down. It was a test of endurance as well as a narrow escape. I rolled up in his hide and kept as warm as if I was in a stove. The hide stretched twelve feet long and eight feet wide when green. Nearly all animals' hides will stretch out longer than the body measurement when stretched as soon as they are skinned.

[*Lilly killed this grizzly, which is probably the only one he bagged in the U.S., at the head of Horton Creek on the east side of Arizona's White Mountains. The site, at an elevation of about 9,000 feet, is near Hannagan Meadow, which, in turn, is about fifteen miles west of the village of Blue. The only part of the bear preserved in the National Museum is the skull, that of an adult male (USNM No. 212436).[21] The specimen has a bullet hole in its underside but is not seriously damaged. It measures 375 millimeters or 14.8 inches in overall length, not 18 inches as Lilly reported.[22] Lilly exaggerated this bear's size in other respects. Male grizzlies in Yellowstone National Park are thought to be somewhat larger than their Southwestern brothers were.[23] Yet they do not achieve lengths anywhere near nine feet. Fifty-five adult males measured during recent studies of Yellowstone grizzlies averaged 77.4 inches from nose to tail following the contour of their backs.[24] A bear nine feet (108 inches) long would likely weigh a ton or more.]*

We may say that the Alma section started the lion-killing of New Mexico in 1912, keeping it up until 1916. It is necessary to say that in 1913 the stockmen made about the same arrangements as the men at Alma, New Mexico, who were extending my hunts from Alma to Luna and as high up as Alpine, Arizona. Only a few of them were offering a bounty. Where there was a bounty paid I hunted from, we will say, the mouth of the Blue River to the head of it. Each section paid for what was killed on its territory. I would work where the worst damage was being done—working everyone's range who was paying. [*Alma, New Mexico, is on the San Francisco River near the western boundary of the state. The village is about sixty miles northwest of Silver City and thirty miles northeast of Clifton, Arizona.*]

I was at Bear Valley, west of Alma, when a man came and told me that bears were killing cattle at the head of Blue River. One big bear had killed fourteen in two weeks. I struck out the next morning. I knew the locality where the killing was done. In two weeks I killed four big male bears and six mountain lions—two large males, two full-grown females, and two half-grown kittens. The lions had killed a young horse and a colt.

I was asked [*by Forest Service officials?*] to tell what the loss of stock was in that locality. I reported that 20 per cent of the young stuff was killed by wild animals—that every fifth calf or colt was caught by bears, lions, or wolves. They wrote me: "Mr. Lilly, we regard you as the closest observer in the field. Why is it that you differ so from all the forest [*Forest Service*] men, who say that 10 per cent is the total death rate?" I answered that I had reference to the rough mountains which had enough wild animals to justify me hunting there. When I reported I had killed seventy-five bears and lions, they wrote me: "You are certainly correct! If we had seventy-five animals [*predators*] to feed [*livestock*], we couldn't feed them on what you claimed [*in fees*]." Many people do not pay bounty because they cannot raise the money. It takes all they make to keep them going.

Most of the time in 1913 was spent between the Blue and Frisco rivers. In that year I hunted but very little east of the Frisco. Later on I took in more territory. I hunted from the head reaches of the Blue on the east side to the south, fifteen miles below Alma, and from the head reaches on the west, south to the mouth of Grant Creek six miles south of Blue post-office. This territory was hunted through several times inside of twelve months.

In 1914 the same territory was worked for lions and bears with equally good or better results. I killed nine mountain lions and three bears in one week. The bears and lions were killing stock. During the latter part of that season the ranchmen all began to pay bounty and to have their sections worked. They could see that it was a good plan—that it was better to pay bounty than to feed the wild animals. I made a good killing in 1914 all through the ranges. Everywhere the bounty was kept up in 1915. I did well, taking in still more territory. The lions were not killing so much stock, neither were the bears, but the people saw they had a chance to get rid of them and they used it. The ranchmen, large and small, kept me busy.

[*Writing in 1938, John D. Guthrie, a former supervisor of Arizona and New Mexico's Apache National Forest (which includes the Blue River watershed), recalled that Ben Lilly worked as a "guard-trapper" on the Apache for a brief time in the early 1910s, prior to being hired by the Biological Survey. Since Ben did not mention being employed by the Forest Service in his discussion of this period in his life, it appears that Guthrie may have been mistaken.*]

In 1916 I did some work for the Biological Survey. I worked over every section I could. No one had any bounty to pay. I made it pretty hard on the lions. They had no protection in that neighborhood [?]. I have worked over the Blue River section from the lower end to its head reaches, both east and west. It is difficult to say just how much stock is destroyed by wild animals. They destroy stock clear to the head reaches of the Frisco River.

I killed a big male lion on the James Brothers' Ranch west of Chloride, New Mexico. I hunted several days around Hermosa and Pankey's Ranch. There were no lions in that section. I caught sight of one near Johnson's Goat Ranch. It was snowed out. Mr. Armour [*evidently Lilly's camp helper*] carried the pack by Chloride to get over to Diamond Bar Ranch, and I footed it [*west*] across the mountains [*the Black Range*]. I lay out in the snow two nights. I found no lion tracks coming over the mountains. Mr. Armour came in, and we came south down Black Canyon. We made a camp in the canyon. I looked around for lions' tracks.

I killed an old she-lion. The dogs treed her. It was pitch-dark. I scrambled down the worst kind of a mountain in the dark and reached the tree that the dogs were barking up. I could not find the lion. It was a medium-sized pine. I finally found a form of something up in the tree. I was shooting a rifle, and when I fired, it jumped high up in the air. It landed somewhere on the ground and ran across Indian Creek. It was getting darker and darker. The lion sprang up a steep bluff and into a tree—a thick and dark spruce tree. I finally made out something that looked different from the other part of the tree and shot at it. Down it came and crossed back over the same creek and treed again. This was a thick spruce tree but in a lighter-looking place. I fired at her again and wounded her very badly. She fell out, and the dogs killed her. I built a big fire and skinned out some meat for the dogs to eat. I had wounded her every shot I made at her in the dark. I found she was suckling young.

[*This hunt took place on a part of the Gila National Forest that soon would be known as the "Gila Wilderness." In 1924 U.S. Forest Service officials decided that a large portion of the upper Gila watershed should remain forever roadless and without industrial development. The Gila Wilderness was the first wilderness area in what is today an extensive federal wilderness-preservation system.*

Ben Lilly's Tales

"Lilley Mountain" and "Lilley Park," features within the Gila Wilderness, were not named for Ben but rather for a man who was killed in the area by Apaches in 1885.[25]]

I found the young the next morning, about half a mile away. They were under a rock—five of them in the bed. The dogs killed one. I skinned the old one and carried the four kittens to camp. Mr. Armour took care of them. We carried them up to the Diamond Bar ranch house. This female lion had three deer covered up in different places. Near where the kittens were there were one cow and two yearlings that she had been eating on—only one at a place.

[*Five kittens in a litter is most unusual, but a mother lion with six kittens has been reported.[26] Researchers working in the San Andres Mountains of southern New Mexico found two, three, and four kittens to be the most common litter sizes there.[27] Lilly often captured mountain lion kittens alive and gave them to ranchers as pets or kept them himself for a while. The ultimate fates of these cats aren't known for sure, but undoubtedly most if not all were destroyed when they became too large to be easily managed. Several photos show Ben with kittens, but none has been found of him with a full-grown pet lion (see Chapter 6). Lilly included captured kittens in his lion kill totals.*]

I was hunting up near where I found the five kittens. It was a bad, dark evening, and it was beginning to snow. I was hunting for a large male lion. I had found his track and thought he was due. It was late Saturday evening. There was a cliff of rocks which this lion passed under when he came along. So I looked and found that he had not been there. As I never hunt or travel on Sunday, I commenced gathering up wood and piling it under this rock. There was not room enough to keep more than two dogs and myself. So I fixed a place for the other two near by. We slept there Saturday night. It snowed Sunday and Sunday night. It was fearfully cold. I had no bedding and kept by the fire to keep alive.

I got out at daylight and found that the big lion had been within twelve feet of where I was lying down by the fire. I had some of the mother lion's meat hanging in a tree to feed the dogs on. I took my axe and swung it on my shoulder. I gathered up my gun and horn. [*When out in the mountains Lilly used a cow's horn to call his dogs to him.*] I had a frying-pan on the fire. I called the dogs out, and they took the lion's track and pulled out. They trailed him down to Black Canyon. He had killed a nice cow that night, eaten off her, and gone on. The dogs traveled much faster than I. They could smell him better after he had filled up on fresh meat. I rushed along all I could and climbed up on the bluffs. I heard the dogs barking, so I hurried on and found they had a female lion treed. She was fixing to jump out. I fired on her and broke her back. Down she came, with the dogs fighting her. I took her entrails out and hung her in up a tree. This female lion could smell where he [*the male lion*] had been eating on the cow and had taken his back track to find it. That is a habit with bears, lions, wolves, dogs, and foxes.

The dogs took the male's track and went on after him. I stayed with the dogs until night. I caught them and tied them up, crawled under a small rock, and built a fire. The next morning the dogs took the lion's track, trailed him about a mile, and jumped another one coming back on his track. They treed her, and I killed her. It was a female with two kittens to be born soon. I took her entrails out and hung her up in a tree.

I then went up to my camp, where Mr. Armour was. He had everything nicely cooked for me. As soon as I had eaten, we went back down and skinned the two lions, staying all night under a rock. The next morning he carried the hides to camp. I went and took the big lion's track and followed it for about six days. I killed him about a mile or two from where we killed and skinned the two females. This large male lion went to several cattle they had been eating on. He seemed to miss the three females that I had killed, and he would go to the cattle they had eaten on.

I searched the ranges very closely for other lion signs. The hounds I use will carry you to a carcass of a calf, colt, deer, or grown stock of any kind if it is covered up. In killing and hunting these nine lions—one old male, three full-grown females, and five kittens—I found [*the cats*] on two ranches that adjoined a line fence which made the difference [*separated the ranches*]—the Diamond Bar and the G.O.S. Ranch. The lions were killed and ranged on both ranges about equally. I found fifteen head of cattle, large and small, that had been killed and eaten by lions.

I then moved to the G.O.S. Ranch, where I killed seven lions and found fifteen head of cattle killed while I was killing the lions. It took about three weeks to kill the seven head on the G.O.S. Ranch.

I have a diary showing that I killed forty-two lions in four months on the G.O.S. and Diamond Bar ranches. This was in 1919. Since the first of September 1920 I have seen but six calves killed by lions. I killed the lion that killed each calf. None of the hunters or cowboys report seeing calves killed by lions although they keep a lookout for that. Mr. Glaze, a wolf-trapper, found one that was killed by a lion. I was away when it was killed. I killed the lion when he took up his traps. I was afraid to work the dogs where the traps were.

[*Most predator hunters used traps or poison to take wolves and coyotes, and many set powerful leg-hold traps for lions and bears. Of course, these methods were a threat to Lilly's dogs, and he could not run his pack safely on ranges where trappers and poisoners were active.*]

It goes to show that by careful work the losses of stock can be stopped. Think of it—7,400 head of cattle run on this range, while lions raise their young on the adjoining ranch! Victor Culberson, manager and one of the owners of the G.O.S. Cattle Company, is the only man who could realize that it would pay to have the lions killed out at once, regardless of cost. He saw that it means money and stock saved to get them killed out, and that the ranch was benefitted by using hounds on the range.

It helps to keep wolves from raising young or moving them to the ranch. I think it is beneficial to ranches to have hounds on it and some man to stay out at night in places where these animals are accustomed to coming in on the ranges. If he visits their bedding-places once in two weeks, they are not apt to stay on that range. Once you get your lions and bears killed out real close, it would be hard to restock that range with the same species from another locality. If the different ranches and stock raisers were to organize and sweep out the animals that do the damage, it would cost but little to keep it up.

These wild animals—say, the large male grizzly bears—have a range of about sixty-five miles. Such a bear is the boss of that section. He will make a trip over the portion that is most suitable for grizzlies to use. He will know where the other grizzlies are feeding and where they are "laying-up" in the daytime. It often happens that he will lie around for a day or so and use the same food they use and then strike out for another family of bears. He will kill a cow or a yearling and eat on it, if it is in a suitable place, for three or four days. Then he will find another family of grizzlies. The other bears smell this meat and blood on him, and they take his back track and go back to the kill and eat it up in this way. The best thing to do is get the large boss males killed first, as they have a tendency to cause the other growing-up animals to get on your range by visiting their kills and help make and eat the kills. At certain seasons they move to different feeding-grounds.

The large boss grizzly, we will say, travels over the bear country once in about two weeks, visiting the places where the bears "lay up" or feed. Sometimes they do not stop but keep on and find another bear and then go on again. Those very old ones make many kills and do not eat a bite of them. Some will stay a day or three days, lie down in sight of their food, eat until it is eaten up, and then go twenty miles in one night, passing through the territory of two or three other bears and not stopping. They generally lie down by themselves and sleep in summer time during hot days. On these trips they have certain dense, thick places where they "lay up." If it is a very old one, you can see where he has as many as a dozen beds. They scratch out holes as deep as half their side and about their length in a dense shade. In the winter they go into a hole in the ground under a rock, which they usually dig. In some regions they go into a cave.

The black bears have the same method of traveling over the range, and their bedding-up is somewhat similar. Their range is usually about forty-five miles. They [*the old males?*] keep watch over the other bears. They rub on trees and bushes at the meeting-places, the same as the grizzlies. There is some difference, yet they are very much alike. Each tribe, if they eat a big bite of meat, will strike out on another range, looking for other bears. Then they will rub on trees and bite on them. In different localities they have different habits. The bears on the Mississippi River and in the big thickets in southern Texas did more biting on trees than those of any other locality I have ever been in. Bears visit the bears' rubbing-places if lost or traveling.

It is well to say here that the male bear is the first to go over the range from one end to the other. If they "lay up" on the south end of the range that he claims, he will strike out for the north end. He seems to be watching on that portion of the mountains, [*to see*] if conditions are favorable. If they prove a failure and there is a chance of their [*the other bears'*] suffering, the large boss makes a move to food in localities which are a suitable home for bears. The female and two-year-olds are the next to follow. It seems that, if the large male leaves and fails to come back, the females with cubs will be the last ones of the bear tribe to move to the same range that he is located on.

These large, very old bears look after the others at all seasons of the year. They make their rounds where the rubbing-places of the different families of bears are. Whether it is the mating season or not, if other bears are passing by these rubbing-places, they will visit them and examine everything very closely. Both sexes and all sizes seem to be glad to rub and play around these rubbing-places. At these places they can find out whether the large bear has killed or eaten on fresh meat. This is done by smelling the bear's breath. There is no other performance left there except rubbing on the tree or biting on it.

[*Present-day authorities do not agree with Lilly's notion that old male bears lead other bears to feeding grounds and thus contribute to their welfare. Bears are not social beasts. Adult males search out females during the breeding season but otherwise live solitary lives (unless unusually rich food sources, such as garbage dumps or salmon runs, bring them into close contact with other bears). In fact, both black and grizzly males will kill cubs if given the chance, and mother bears avoid contact with the big males until their cubs are grown and they are again ready to mate.[28]*]

The mountain lion makes two strokes with the front foot in the dust or straw six to ten inches long and six or seven inches wide. The straw will usually be about five to seven inches at the back part where his foot stops. This performance is carried on by the male when he has made a kill and is hunting other lions. This is called "pawing." [*There are various names for the marks made by the*

Bears and Lions

pawing of male lions—"scrapes," "scratches," "markers," etc.] Females do not use that performance—it is used only by males. All traveling lions visit these place when they get lost from the other lions, large or small.

[*Writer Kevin Hansen states that male lions make "scrapes" with "either the forepaws or hindpaws." Researchers working in southern New Mexico during the period 1985-1995 reported that male lions make scrapes with their hind feet. However they make them, they are believed to mark the largely exclusive "home ranges" of adult male lions—the scrapes inform other males that the area is occupied. Occasionally a resident tom will urinate or defecate on the pile of debris, reinforcing his claim to the area with his scent.*[29]]

The very old male mountain lions have very nearly the same habits as bears. They travel through the ranges of lions and visit all the different lions that are in that locality—all sizes and sexes. They usually raise two sets of kittens in about twelve or fifteen months.

[*Modern experts maintain that adult male mountain lions are very solitary animals and do not socialize with other lions except when mating.*[30] *Large males sometimes kill smaller lions, and vulnerable young lions are wise to stay clear of them.*[31] *And, again, female mountain lions raise one litter every eighteen to twenty-four months, not two litters in twelve to fifteen months.*[32]]

Bears raise cubs but once in two years. The cubs are usually born in February and are said to be the smallest babies of any animal in proportion to the mother's size. The bear has been known to bring four, and the lion has been found with five. As a rule, the lion brings from one to three, and the bear the same number. There are exceptions occasionally.

It would be quite a pleasure to me to describe the habits of all the wild animals as I understand them—the males, the females, and the youngsters at birth and until fully grown. This article does not attempt to describe any but the mountain localities where bears and lions were very plentiful. It would be difficult for a man who has not had the time and opportunity to realize as facts the things I am trying to explain. You surely can see from the number of bears and lions that I have killed since 1908 what it would take to feed them, and you can see from the pains that Mr. Culberson took that they can be killed out. The only way is to have them killed out close. It would be a good thing to have young men take up hunting, search their own locality first, and then try an unknown region to see if it would assist them in getting familiar with the wild animals' habits. Wild animals act differently when they are very scarce. The loss from predatory animals is very heavy in some localities in the rough mountain country which are suitable for bears and lions.

2

MOUNTAIN LIONS OF NEW MEXICO

by Ben V. Lilly

Editor's note: Precisely when Ben Lilly wrote the following discourse on mountain lions isn't known, but he was up in years when he composed it. Frank Dobie included a condensed and highly-polished version in his book *The Ben Lilly Legend* (1950). Here Lilly's original, rough-hewn essay is published in its entirety for the first time. As readers will see, Ben had an informal approach to spelling and punctuation.

◇ ◇ ◇ ◇ ◇

New Mexico has localities making an ideal home for mountain lions. The portion of the State that I have found where they Seemed to be the thickest during all Seasons of the year is in the South Western portion of the State. They mostly inhabit the Highest roughest of mountains and rove from the Valleys and rough canions to the Very highest mountains and roughest ledges of rocks and cliffs to lay up in day time. In freazing weather they after catching and eating their catch or a part of it will cover it up with leaves trash and dirt. Then they often travel to a drink of water and move to Some place where the Sun Shines against the big rocks and warms up the air. They often get under Some thick under brush and make a Small flat bed on dry leaves or Straw. In Some few cases they will Stay 12 or 24 hours then go back to the Same carcas and eat and Select another beding place and eat again from the Same carcas before leaving. The habits I have Just explained would apply to the mountain lion of about one year old male or female.

The female old or young that is raising young will often commence Killing and covering up Such food as they will need. They make the Kill drag it to Some thick under brush or log or rock and cover it up with trash leaves or bark and Some dirt. It is Safe to Say they commence this about 2 weeks before the little fellows is born. They usually have beds made at the most Suitable place near the Kills Say in a mile or So of Some of the Kills. The litter usually Varies in number from 1 to 4. I once took five from 1 bed. I have took 1 from about 2 young Mothers first Kits to be born and I Killed one Very old female with one Kitten yet to be born Soon. I find that 2 Kits to the first litter the Mothers bring and 3 Kits after the first is born. I have found 4 Kits yet to be born in 6 different Mother lions. It is a Very rare thing to find 4. I find that the female lion of South West New Mexico brings young in any one of the 12 months during a year. I have found them yet to be born at all Seasons of the year. They often raise 2 Sets of Kittens in 12 or 15 months. It is a Very common thing to find unborn at any Season of the year. I think in real good years the Mother will Save five Kittens in 12 or 15 months.

[*Female mountain lions raise one litter of kittens every eighteen to twenty-four months or thereabouts. As for litter size, researchers working in the San Andres Mountains of southern New Mexico during the years 1985-1995 reported four-kitten litters to be rather common. They also found first litters to be larger than subsequent ones.[33]*]

When the little Kittens are born they are about the Size of a rat and Spotted. Black [*spots*] yellowish [*background*]. Spots all over their backs and Sides and on the front part of their legs. Their face and body has Some Strips and Small Spots. Their eyes are deep blue when open. That is in about 9 days after birth. They grow Very fast and make a nice little pet. The Mother continues to go out and Kill Such food as She can find and wants and when they are 8 or 9 days old She will usually Stay at night with them and Start out in the evening about 3 oclock and come back after dark. As they grow older She Stays out longer and at about 3 or 4 months the Mother moves them to the Kills She makes and covers up. The Mother will rove off in Search of food about 7 miles away from the young.

The food they Kill mostly in South West N. Mex. is Sheep goats deer calves cows colts and horses. I have caught the young and chained the young where She left them eating on a deer calf or colt. She would come back that night but would be gone the next day. I would put 2 hounds on her track and tie one hound to me thinking I might find another young one that might have escaped while I was tieing the one I captured. The dog[s] would take the track I and the other dog following.

[*Lilly hunted on foot and could not cover the ground as quickly as a horseman. Therefore, his dogs often would get out of hearing when trailing a lion or bear. Lilly could follow the dogs' tracks, but this was slow and a rain might wash them out. In order to help locate a hard-running pack that had gotten far ahead, Lilly would keep a "guide" dog tied to his waist. The leashed dog followed the others by scent and was able to hear their barking at a much greater distance than its master could. Ben had become deaf in one ear before he left Louisiana. Thus he had difficulty determining the direction a sound was coming from—a serious handicap in working with trail hounds. Consequently, guide dogs were as important to Ben's hunting success as the dogs trailing the game.*]

We found things She would Kill and cover up. It would be Very interesting to See their method of Slipping up on the animals they wanted to catch. I find that they go about 7 miles away from their young and Kill about 3 animals a yearling a colt and a deer. This is when their young is large enough to move them to their Kill. They Seem to give the Situation the benefit of the move not the Variety of meat. I think the Mother moves them to the places that is Safest for the young where there is water near and rough rocks and good hiding places for the young. Young lions drink lots of water. Older ones drink Very little. When She leaves them at food and water they go to water themselves.

I have trailed them in the Snow with myself and dogs. The little ones runs on logs and climbs trees runs on rocks. If there is 3 Kittens at times one will follow its Mother and 2 Kits will branch off to them Selves and all get together as they travel along in the Snow. I have followed them about 8 miles and they had only Stopped once. She lay down under Some rocks and they played all around her. She was giveing milk. She had Killed 2 Sheep and was carrying them to it. I caught and made pets of two of the Kits. Killed the Mother and

1 Kit.

They leave their young to eat where they are and then the Mother goes far off and eats from one of her Kills that was made Several days [*before*]. I have Known them to make a fresh Kill after leaving the young. Then the Mother would not eat a mouth ful of it. Would cover it up good and go to Some carcas that they had Killed 8 or 10 days before and eat on it. It Seems as though they are careing for their young in this way. The lion tries to Select a cool place to hide and cover it up in Summer months. In winter and in time of Snow Storms they will cover their Kills up with trash and Snow and if it freezes hard they will often go and Kill Something else. They use a fresh Kill in frozen wether.

The Kitten lions usually Shed off the first Kitten coat of hair at from 4 to 7 months old and then the Spots disappear. The food and way they are cared for has a great deal to do with the time they Shed off. If they are growing fast and fat they will Shed quicker. If badly treated the Spots will remain longer. After the Spots are gone their color will be the Same as the full grown ones and at about this age the new tusks of teeth Starts that remains the balance of their lives. Their color Varies in diferent localities. If they are in the high mountains and Very fat the Mother lion that travels in day time in Search of food would get poor. She would be a Shade lighter than a fat one that travels only at night and Stayed fat and lay up in the Shade during the day. The males are usually the darkest even when raised as pets. The female Kittens Seems to be more cross than the male when raised as pets. To get real Kind pets they Should be caught before they become attached to their Mother. I never Saw a family of Kittens that was all of one Sex. There is male and female with ever family I ever found.

The male mountain lion of New Mexico he is a little larger than its Sister at birth and 3 months old you can See that he will have a little braver motion as he moves and She will be cross and cautious at the Same age. I can realize that it is her nature to develope caution and care for Self protection at an earlier age than he. He is inclined to be brave and daring and inderpendant. This is nature and they inhirit their Share from their parents. This little male lion and Sister will be up early in the morning. They will watch the movement of the Skies and Surroundings. Then they watch every bird and anything that moves and want to go. They will try to catch any thing their Size. They will catch chickens or fowls or what they can get in reach of. They are natural hunters and no doubt would make a living at a Very early age as hunger would learn them to catch frogs lizards grasshopers. Their Mother feeds them on the choicest of food but in captivity they Show their inclination to hunt for themselves. I once Saw where three half grown ones Killed a 2 months old calf. I Killed all three of them. They had traveled 3 days without food. I found nothing they had eat on.

The male lion travels and hunts with the family he is raised with. If there is 2 or 3 Kittens raised together they are apt to Stay together. At about 5 to 7 months they Shed their Kitten teeth and at about 5 months they are wened. [*Zoologists have found that mother mountain lions wean their kittens when they are two to three months of age.*[34]] Their Mother still Kills for them after being wened and they eat on the Same carcases as one family. The Kittens are great Killers. At 8 to 10 months old they are playful and great Killers on Small deer and young Stock. They often double up. All of the youngsters Jump on the Same animal. I have Seen where they bit and choked them to death. The larger lions Kills them instantly. When the young is about 9 months or 11 old She [*their mother*] moves away from them and in 2 or 3 months She is in charge of another bunch of Kittens. These year old lions will Kill and She will eat on their Kill or they will eat on her Kill. When the last Kittens is about 4 months old She doesnt care for the year old any longer unless the last Kittens are destroyed. This would make the first Kittens about 12 months old.

[*Contemporary authorities contend that female lions do not remain in close contact with their grown offspring, do not share kills with them, etc., after a new litter is born. Mountain lions are not gregarious animals, and, except when mating, mature adults have little to do with each other.*[35]]

Then the male begins to travel Some to himself in Search of other lions and returning to the Section he was raised in. I have Seen where he would make a Kill and drive a female 12 miles to where he had Killed a young Steer. It was getting dark when we found the Kill. I had 2 dogs trailing the lions and one on a line to help me with

Ben Lilly's Tales

the trailing dogs. We found the male lion near the Kill. I Shot him 2 Shots on the run and wounded him each Shot at a distance of 300 yards. The dogs found him laying under Some rock after dark. I Shot him again. This was Saturday night. I went to the nearest water and I Stayed all day Sunday on the Spot. Monday I went and trailed the female about 8 or 9 miles and about 11 oclock I Killed her.

These males doesnt always do that way. I was trailing a large male once and he had Killed a grown cow and eat off of it and Kept on. There was Snow on the ground and after trailing the male 2 miles the hounds treed a female lion that was coming back on his track to find the cow and I Killed her. I tied her up in a tree and didnt wait to Skin her. Her intrels was took out. I took the males track where the dogs turned off after the female lion they had treed and I had Killed. The dogs took the male lions track and followed it until dark. I caught and tied them up. I lay under a rock all night. I Kept fire all night. Didnt have nothing to cook. I took the hounds to where I caught them up and they took the big male lions track that they was trailing and I right after them. They went about 2 miles and met a female lion that was coming back on the male lions track. I Kept up with them. They Soon treed her. I Killed her and hung her up in a tree. Took her intrals out and went to a camp I had about 7 miles away.

I found here a man. Plenty cooked to eat. As Soon as I finished eating we come back where I had the two lions hanging up which was 4 miles apart. I Skinned the first one Killed then went on to the Second one and I Skinned it. It was Sundown and Snow everywhere. We gathered wood and made big fire and Stayed all night. Next morning the man went to camp with the hides and I went after the big lion that I was trailing. The two hounds and I trailed him 4 days and I Killed hem in about 4 miles from where that last female was Killed. She was about one year old and was carrying 2 well developed Kittens that would have arrived in about two weeks.

The first female I hung up was giving milk. She must have been giving milk for about 3 weeks. All of her tits was full of milk and I would Say She was the Mother of three Kittens. [*Mountain lions have eight teats but apparently only six produce milk.*[36]] In this case the male lion met the first one and She Smelled the blood and fresh meat and took his back track to find the dead cow he had Killed. The younger lioness the last one I Killed was coming back on his track the 2nd day after the cow was Killed. She had Struck his track and no doubt Smelt the fresh meat and was going to the Kill he made for food. Animals Know how to go back on tracks to find the food.

This is not intended for a lion Story. Yet to get at the habits and ways of these animals it I hope is not out of place to State facts from experience with these animals. The first animal explained as a male lion about one year old drove what was Supposed to be the Sister of Same age 12 miles to where he had Killed a year old Steer. She had Killed a calf and had eat it up the most of it leaving only a few pieces buried there and he drove her to where he had Killed a better animal and they was Killed by me. As I explained also I Killed the old male that Killed the cow and the 2 females that has tracked his back track expecting to find the food.

[*Field biologists have not discovered evidence suggesting that male mountain lions "drive" females to kills or anywhere else. Nor have researchers found evidence that female mountain lions backtrack males by scent to find their kills in the manner described by Lilly. Adult female lions are fully capable of hunting for themselves. Furthermore, mountain lions do not have an especially keen sense of smell—theirs is less acute than that possessed by canines and bears. Lions hunt primarily by sight and do not rely on their noses to find food.*[37]]

The old male differs from the young in this way. He usually makes a Kill and Strikes out through the places where he expects to find other lions. He usually eats 2 or 3 times before he leaves the Kill. In Some cases he will lay down and rest at the Kill under Some thick brush or rock or old logs. Cover it up and go after water and be back again about the 3rd or 4th day from the time he made his Kill. He usually Strikes out to where other lions uses Varying in direction acording to the Variation of the country. If there is rough cliffs and high rugged mountains and caves and creveses where other lions lays up in day time he is apt to travel on the tops of these bluffs. And wherever there is dry trash and dry Straw he will Stop and take 2 Strokes with his front foot. This will leave a place about 8 to 12 inches long and about 7 inches wide. If the Straw or trash is Very deep it will be about 3 inches high at the back where the foot Starts.

There is usually no other performance carried on there. This is done when they are full of food and in Search of other lions or traveling. If this Same lion comes through there again he will Visit this Same place and paw up the Straw in Same way again Somewhere within 2 or 3 foot of the first work. He is apt to have a dozen pawing places in about 15 miles travel. They will travel as far as 15 miles in one night when they are hunting other lions. They Scarcely ever paw up Straw when they are hunting food. The females and young lions male or female Visits these points or pawing places. The young male will paw in the Straw even tame at about 4 months old. The female rarely ever paws. Yet they go to these points when traveling. When they are hunting Something to catch they rarely go near them.

They Search for deer calves and colts. They will Kill a grown cow or a full grown horse or mule. They prefer a colt Say 2 to 4 months old. They like a calf about 3 or 4 months old best. They Seldom Kill a Very poor animal of any Kind. If they Kill any one that is not fat their preference would be a deer. The food I have found in their Stomachs was Deer Cattle Horses Goats Sheep Hogs. Of the 6 Varieties booth Kinds [*sexes?*] were Killed. Young and old burros and mules are Killed in Some localities. I have found porcupine [*and*] Skunk and I found 2 cotton tailed rabbits in lions Stomach one in each lions Stomach. They were female lions about 9 months old and Killed in different locations in New Mexico. I found one with a grouse in its Stomach and a year later I found another with a grouse in its Stomach. It is Very plain to See that the Ranches Suffer Great losses from mountain lions in the localities they inhabit in New Mexico Say the roughest high mountains in the South West Side.

The large male mountain lions is the one of the lion family that makes his trips over the mountains in Search of food conditions and other lions. He Kills what Suits him. Eats what he wants. Covers up his Kill. Usually goes to water. Lays up at a Suitable place. Comes back to his Kill. Eats and cover it up and goes on in Search of other lions taking in his travels. When he meets other lions Say the day he eat the meal 12 hours before he met another lion they will be Very hungry [*and*] drift back to that food. Or if one Strikes his track they will Know by the Sent of him that he has had fresh meat and if they are Very hungry they may Stay at that carcas for a day or So. He will make his rounds again in about 14 days. This means if neither he or the lions has not been bothered or the animals he is Killing have not changed their range. He wants to See if other lions has been as his Kill. They Seldom ever eat on a carcas after they Start in Search of other lions but make a new Kill.

It is Safe to think that this lion learned this from his Mother at an age of 4 to 6 months old. At that age She goes away and makes a Kill and then moves them to it. They Stay and eat it up. As Soon as they are filled up She Strikes out and makes another Kill Some times 2 or 3 in one night. She comes back and moves them to where She likes best and leaves them. The lions Killing drives the wild animals on. Of course they go to the next best feeding place. That is the Deer cows and horses drift towards home or the best feeding grounds. This causes the Mother lion to move her young to Such places that they can make a living off of her Kills and by the time the Kittens is nine or 12 months old they Know the ranges of mountains and the domestic and wild animals that can be caught and eat and not endanger their lives. In this way the old males are the leaders. His first lessons were learned from his Mothers care and protection. Then his task is to Visit the ranges Just as far as it is a desirable country for lions to live in and take care of the ones he has left behind him. The male lion is the first one to Start out on Search to See the best place for his food. Then the barren Shes and year olds follow Kind of drifting over the Same direction. He goes and if he makes Kills they eat them. What I mean by Baron Shes is females that has no Kittens at that time. Then the Mothers and Kittens are usually the ones that are behind. She is usually 2 months Slower in getting over the range. She will carry them over the range before the Season is over and maybe back to wean them and raise another family in that locality. Most all lions have certain routes they prefer traveling on.

[*Present-day investigators do not share Lilly's belief that adult male mountain lions help other lions by leading them to hunting grounds and by willingly sharing their kills with them. Adult mountain lions do not feed together. They are solitary hunters, and, unlike African lions, each mature adult must find and kill its own prey. Yes, mountain lions will occasionally feed on carcasses of animals they did not kill, but they do not make a habit of eating carrion. And, while adult males expend considerable effort seeking out females in breeding condition, they ignore those that are not ready to mate. Mature lions of both sexes establish more or less exclusive "home ranges" where they live and hunt. The home range system has several functions, but mainly it spreads the cats out and prevents crowding and lessens competition for prey and mates. An old tom's home range will overlap those of several females and may overlap a portion of an adjacent male's territory. But, for the most part, the home ranges of male lions are avoided by other males. Thus the home range scheme reduces the chance of a dangerous physical encounter between adult males, and a resident male can breed with the females in his preserve without undue interference. The big toms have been known to kill and eat smaller lions, and immature males and females with kittens give the old males a wide berth. In short, except for mating, adult male lions live apart from others of their kind.[38]]*

Mountain lions is Very destructive on live Stock and deer. I made a trip for the Biological Survey of Washington D.C. on Predatory animals in March 1917. I was hunting on Diamond Bar Ranch managed by Mr. H. L. Hodge and G.O.S. Ranch managed by Mr. Victor Culberson. In 2 weeks I Killed 9 lions and in the Same time in trailing these lions I found 15 head of cattle the lions had Killed and eat off of. I moved over the G.O.S. Ranch and Killed 7 lions and in trailing the 7 lions I found 15 head of cattle that the lions had Killed and eat off of. This was done in 1917. This had been a Very hard winter and the lions drove down by the Snow. This Killing was done in about 15 or 20 miles Square or rather longer on Some points. I Set the numbers down as I found them. There is but few Persons who Know they do So much destruction to Stock. They Kill in localities where men cant ride and hide them in bad rough localities.

As to the Measurment of Mountain Lions in New Mexico Full Grown Males measures from end of nose to end of tail 7 foot to 7 foot 6 inches. Females average 6 foot 8 inches and 6 foot 3. One Killed went to 7 foot 5 inches. Yearling males run about 6 foot 4 inches. Yearling females run about 5 foot 9 inches. Their length and Size Varies in even the Same mountains and ranges that they are raised in. Most all animals grow larger and faster where they get choice food and lots of it. It is Safe to Say that most animals grow a little faster and larger in a level damp country than in a Very dry high altitude. I think the high altitude Grows firmer forms yet not quite as large as the lower lands with equal amount of food.

It is a Very difficult task to get correct measurments of wild animals. In the first place one must feel the responsibility that he is authority on that line or He will get careless in measuring and fail to write the measurement down on paper. The correct way is to measure the animal from the end of the nose to the end of the tail laid out perfectly Strait before Skinning. Then measure from the bottom of front foot to the top of Shoulder. Do the Same on hind foot from the bottom of the foot to top of hip directly over the bottom as though the animal was Standing up Straight. Then measure from the end of tail to where it Joins the bodye. That gives you the length and Higth and the length of tail. Now measure length of hind foot.

The hide when Skinned off will Stretch out about 3 feet longer than the measurements of a full grown lion if hide is not allowed to dry any. Skinned and Stretched while it is Still warm and Stretched the long way first then Stretch the Sides out. It is best not to over stretch a hide. This is mentioned to give a chance to protect the man who asks how long was your lion? So many feet and So many inches. The next question is hide measure or measured from end of nose to end of tail? Hide measurement is not correct as the Stretch that is in different hides would give different results. A Very old and large lion hide would be tough and if the least dry would not Stretch.

In collecting for the museum at Washington D.C. I heard of one place in Texas where there had been lions Killed that measured 13 feet long. I was planning to try to get one of them for the Biological Survey. I had Sent them a big fellow from Old Mexico that measured 8 feet nine and a half inches long body measurement. I hunted up the Texas man that measured the famous hide. He was a carpenter. He Says to me I will get the book. I am the man that measured it and we will See what it is. As it read 7 foot long that broke that hunt up. The man that told me was Sure that the lion was 13 feet long.

We are not correct on unknown Subjects every time. For

instance you tell a lion hunter the distance between 2 Stars is 5 light days. Ask him what the distance was and I dare Say he couldnt remember 2 figures. These things are all mentioned in order to try and get the proper facts about the Mountain lions of New Mexico. I can only Speak of what I Know in a brief way and it will no doubt give you a platform to stand on to Start in Search of what you would want to Know about lions and their ways in the State.

I have been from the South Western Border to the head reaches of the Pacos [*Pecos*] River and the Head reaches of the Rio Grande River. They Seem to give trouble to the Stock raisers in each portion. If they are plentiful the damage is much worse. I feel quite Sure that a full grown lion will Kill 2 animals in ten days the Size of a deer or larger. They may be Killed 20 miles apart if it is an old male. The female with young Kills as many as 3 in one night at certain ages of the young ones about 4 or 6 months old. They dont eat on them all but Kill and cover up. They go out most every day or two and Kill when they can find Some thing that Suits them. If it is in extreme hot weather the Blow flies Soon ruins the extra Kill and if it is in extreme cold it will freeze and they will make another Kill rather than eat on frozen meat. Other animals large and Small helps to destroy the food. Buzards at times coyotes and wolves and bob cats Visits their Kills and eats on them.

    I was trailing a large old male Grizzly bear and he began to take an entire different course. I was using a Slow track hound that never got out of reach of me. The dog Swung directly South over ledge of rocks down in a Small canion and finally went through Some fine Sand and this Big grizzly was back tracking a large male lion. We followed close for a while and commenced zig zaging right left and South. He climbed up over a cliff of rocks and thick brush and then he found a large buck deer that this male lion had Killed and covered up. The grizzly ate it up. Lay down at the carcass. Eat up the Scraps and pulled out the Same direction he was going. This Bear could tell from the Sent that the lion had Killed a deer and he Knew how to find it by following his back track and when he began to zig zag he Smelled the deer himself and went to it without following the lions tracks.

    In 1912 I was up from Animas N.M. about 40 miles north of the

Lang place on the Border Known as Diamond A Ranches. I was Killing bear and lions West and North of Almer [*Alma*] New Mexico on Hugh McKeen Ranch and Joining ranches. I Killed Six bear and 4 lions in 2 weeks. I met a man who was a prospector and he told me that he Saw a leopard on [*Big*] Dry creak [*about ten miles southeast of Alma*] about a year ago and described his color to me and I told him I guessed it was a Jaguar and I would give him $10.00 if he would find a track of this animal and cover it up So I could See his Size. I told him all I wanted was a track. I Saw the man 2 or 3 times afterwards. He Said he couldnt find no track or hear of none.

I Kept on Killing bear and lions. In the first 5 months I Killed 47 bear and lions. The next year I Killed 48 Bear and lions. The first year I Killed about as many of each. The Second year I Killed more lions than bear. This hunting was did mostly in New Mexico not more than 10 miles east of the Arizona line and I hunted in Arizona not more than 10 miles west of the New Mexico line. The hunting was good on each Side. One Side equalled the other back as far as I went. I was hunting for bounty from the Ranchers and as they [*the bounties*] began to get Scarce I took in larger territory.

The Second year there was reported that there was a man in Clifton Arizona who Killed a Leopard in the red mountains about 45 [*30*] miles North of Clifton 30 [*20*] miles west of Alma New Mexico. This man was hunting deer and Shot the Jaguar and wounded him badly and when he reached the place where he Saw it Struggling he was Frightened to find a full grown Jaguar Struggling trying to get away. The Jaguar had Killed a deer. Mr. Tol [*Toles*] Cosper who lived about 15 miles North on the Blue River Showed me the Skull. It was a male. Old one.

There is a bone that grows as age advances on the top of the Skull on male animals and as they grow older it gradually grows higher. It first Starts at the back of the Skull and gradually grows higher and Straight on top of the Skull. It doesnt get as far up as even with the eyes. It grows on the center of the back of the Skull to about half or two thirds of the way to even between the eyes. It is confined to the center of the Skull. It grows as high as a half inch high on an old male lion and it will gradually go forward until it grows out even with the top of the Skull. The bear and lions and all of the males of the cat tribe has it and all of the bear Species and dogs even Squirrels. It only appears on old males. It doesnt Show on young animals or female. I found a few real old female lions with the least appearance of it on their Skulls. [*This structure, known as the "sagittal crest," is the upper-rear part of the cranium, not a separate bone.*]

The Jaguar Showed he was a real old fellow. The young man who Killed it Sent it to McFadun Denver Colorado and had it made into a rug with full head open mouth. It was real nice. It was almost a dark yellow color. Very light for a Jaguar. The usual black Spots were as usual in round dots 7 rows to a Side. The Spots about the hind and front of legs was nice. I looked it over closely. This was in 1913 I Saw it and from the description the man gave me of the animal he Saw on Dry creek in New Mexico it must have Spent Some time in the Dry creek country. They Said it had been Seen and its tracks were there up to 1911 any way but no one Saw his tracks after I offered $10.00 for one track.

I hunted in the red mountain country [*in eastern Arizona*] in 1915 and 1916. Killed Several lions but found no trace of lepards. It is my opinion this one was the one that Stayed on the Dry creek in New Mexico. There had been a leopard Killed South east of the Anamas [*Animas*] Mountains. This I was told [*was*] in 1909 and I was told they chased one that got away. It had been Several years Since these were Killed and chased. Any way one had been Killed at or near a place called Dog Springs in New Mexico. I hunted in the Animas mountains and Old Mexico. I found and Killed 13 lions Some nice grizzlies and 12 bear. I found no leopards or Jaguars on either Side.

New Mexico is real nice locality for mountain lions. The roughest mountains is well watered and most of the roughfest mountains has well fed cattle and lots of them. There is many deer roaming wild on the large ranches. It has its Share of wild turkeys. It also has Several Varietys of fur bearing animals. There is mountain lions and bear both to be found in northern New Mexico at the ranges of mountains connected with the head reaches of the Pacos [*Pecos*] River and the head reaches of the Rio Grande river up to the Colorado line. I found the South West has Sections of mountanous countries that gives them excellent food and protection from civilization. But with So much Stock being raised and the wild game to raising each year [?] and Settle ments is Slowly driving them toward the roughfest mountains. The deep Snows and cold winds will force them to Search the roughest mountains to get the best food. The South Slopes and brush that ocurs on ranches that is not over Stocked with cattle is the Sections that they will Kill the most cattle on. There has been a good year as Stock is fat in most Sections.

In 1912 and 1913 I made a Statement that I thought the bear and lions was Killing 20 per cent of the young Stock in the rough country I was hunting in. That meant every fifth calf or colt was Killed by bear or lions or wolves. They wrote back to me and Said Mr. Lilly we regard you as the closest observer in the field. How is it you Vary So much from the other men in the forest? I wrote them I had reference to the location that was good enough to Justify my hunting in. Rough mountains. They Said you Say twenty percent of the young Stuff and the others all Say ten percent death rates. Animals dying [*naturally*] and animals Killed combined. As Soon as I had Killed 75 bear and lions they wrote back to me. You are Shurely correct. If a man had to feed 75 bear and lions he couldnt do it at your figures and we Know how much is wasted when they feed themselves. Up to that time there was no way of Knowing the number of animals was living on cattle and other domestic animals. Both the bear and lions Kills animals [*including*] cows horses and Sheep and goats hogs.

The thing that is So hard for a man to believe is that the lion will Kill and travel So far away from its Kill to make another Kill. At other times they will make Kills and Stay near the Same locality for Several weeks and Seem to be at home and then Start out on a Stroll of Several days and not be heard of no more for a whole Season then return to Same locality again. Most all wild animals try to take a roving trip about twice a year in the early Spring and early Fall as a general rule. This is not a rule but a habit. They are made to look after different Kinds of food. The old males would look after food and Keep trace of the other lions and the female with Small young would Kill and travel acording to what the young was able to Stand. The baron Shes and yearling will try to Keep with the deer colts calves goats and Sheep as food. The food has a great deal to do with their trips yet they try to Select the best food. In a rough mountainous locality the rough rocks and caves cliffs and ledges give good hiding places for the older ones and younger ones that is coming on. The Mother Seems to try to take their young over the entire range when She is about ready to weane them or when they are about 9 months old. It often ocurs that the Mother will eat on a carcas or Kill with the yearlings when She has younger Kittens in a bed near by and I have Seen where these year old Kittens would Visit the younger Kittens. The old Mother Seldom ever eats off of the food that She moves the young to. Will eat off of a Killing She makes far away from them. The Mother in coming back to the Kittens at 4 or 5 days old or a month old will always Slip out and in from a diferent direction to avoid making a trail by which their enemies could locate their young.

[*Mountain lion kittens are weaned from their mother's milk when they are two to three months of age. The kittens commonly stay with their mother for at least twelve months and sometimes as long as eighteen months, then they go off to establish home ranges of their own. Mother lions do not socialize with their grown offspring after they have given birth to a new litter—one does not encounter three generations of mountain lions feeding together, etc.[39]*]

In November 1912 I Saw a female lion track while I was trailing a grizzly bears track that had been gone about 6 days. The lion had been gone about 8 days going South. 2 young lions following her about a year old. The old one made a track with left front foot that Showed five toes on the track. They was traveling South. This was found on Foot [*Foote*] Creak in Arizona 8 miles west of Blue river and Blue Post office and about 10 or 12 miles West of the Arizona line. This was Saturday evening. I followed the big grizzly to where he took the large male lions back track and found the large buck deer the lion had Killed and covered up. The Bear ate the Deer and lay up a day and finished up the balance of the deer and Struck out in the direction of the high mountains on the Blue range at the head reaches of Foot Creak. I found 3 more lion tracks late that evening going South. The bear continued going West. These three lions Seemed to be 3 year olds. They had been gone 5 or 6 days. It was late Saturday evening and I never hunt on Sunday So I came back to a camp and lay over in camp Sunday. It Snowed all Saturday night and all tracks was all put out.

Mr. E. H. Golley of El Paso Texas was out with me. He Killed 2 lions both large females a number of turkeys and Several nice Buck deer. His time was due at El Paso Texas. We gave up the hunt for the big bear and he Started for home February 1914 [*1913?*]. I found the female lions track with five toes on left front foot going South [*cats normally leave four-toed tracks*]. It was 30 miles South of where I first Saw it and I followed her track and two other lions that was traveling with her I thought was her yearlings. I went 30 miles more on their tracks and a big Snow Stoped the tracking. They were 3 or 4 days ahead of me and never made a Stop. I inquired of all the hunters if any of them had Killed her or found her tracks. Couldnt hear a thing of her nor her track. I had hunted over the ranges time and again on the Blue River on both Sides from a few miles above the mouth to the head reaches of it. I had hunted the Frisco River a little above the mouth of the Blue River to the head reaches of the Apachie [*White*] Mountains on the West.

I was hunting on the Saliece [*Saliz Mountains*] South of Reserve [*New Mexico*] for the Biological Survey in 1916 on Mr. Barbers and Dr. Depps ranch. I trailed an old She and 2 yearlings one evening. A man and his Son was out with me. We Set up all night by a fire. The next morning I turned the hounds loose and we Soon took the trail and Killed 3. An old Female and 2 yearlings. That night the man asked me how far does a lion travel? My answer as far as the ranges Suits it. I called his attention to the five toed track I Saw in 1912. I went out the next day and Struck this five toed lions track. Trailed all of one evening and Killed her about dark. She proved to be the one that made a track with 5 toes on it and this was caused by a trap. I guess the toe was pulled out of Joint and the point of the toe pulled out to the outside made one track So that the Stub left there made a track representing five toes.

When I Killed her I took her back track the next day from where I first Started it to See if She was hunting food or Just traveling. I Saw Scar on her of a deers horns fresh and her Stomach was empty. That would lead me to believe She had Killed a deer and did not get to eat it and I might find that another lion had took her deer away from her. I could Kill him if I found his track. I trailed her about 6 miles back and found where She had Jumped on a Very large buck deer and they had both lost a lot of hair in a low thick rough Scrubby thicket. They tore down and broke brush for 15 or 20 feet in diferent directions. I think the deer Scrapped her loose by dashing her against the thick brush. The last place he bounded through was too thick for the lion to remain on the deer and the Scars made on the lion was made with deers horns. This lion Seemed to have raised young that Season yet there was no indication of young. I would rather think her young had been destroyed and She was traveling to get away from the locality. She was heading in the direction where I found her tracks in Arizona in 1912. She was Killed in New Mexico in 1916. I Saw her tracks one hundred miles apart. From where She was Killed to where I Saw her tracks last in Arizona is a little over one hundred miles apart. It would be hard for me to Say where She had been during that time.

[*Ben Lilly often overestimated distances. The Foote Creek/Blue River region in Arizona, where Lilly followed a five-toed lion track in 1912, is about thirty miles west of the Saliz Mountains in New Mexico, where he killed a cat with a similar track four years later.*]

I have caught and raised Several pet lions and bear and will Say that they are Safest with one master. One can be raised as Kind as a house cat Kitten and apparently perfectly gentle and in 2 days he or She could be Spoiled So it would not be Safe. The ones that use pet lions after they are grown or two years old Should Know the nature of animals and have Self control or he will be taking chances of ruining his pet. They are easily tamed if handled right when young. Think of it. All animals that Mothers give it its liberty at Say 6 months old and is not fed with the Mothers milk any more and is at liberty to plunge on its meats at will and has that to do to exhist is likely to become a little unruly in captivity.

And each year the wild tribe is getting wilder and wilder. As civilization moves forward they are driven back in Search of exhistance. I am inclined to think that the reason that tame wild animals doesnt thrive and grow the Same in captivity as in the wilds is the young Should have the Same Kind of food occasionally as the Mother lived on before they were caught even though they were ever So Small when caught. No doubt the Same line of food She lived on would give more Strength and activity to them than Some food you could get them to eat and no doubt would not Sustain the Same amount of energy and growth.

Most all animals after eating fresh meat that is raised on grass as Soon as they get hungry they want green grass. They will in Some cases refuse bread and eat green grass and often through it up. This is on the Same principal as the man who eat a hearty meal of fresh fish. As Soon as his System becomes thoroughly under the influence of the fish and that begins to leave the Stomach in a perishing condition he craves water. The water is required for his Stomach on the Same principal that the fish had to have it to live on. The animals that eat deer cattle and horses I find wants green Vegetation. Grass wheat oats rye Sprouts or other green Vegetation that the animal they eat on ate in his life. The wild animal Searches and finds tender Vegetation in damp places that is tender and young. While they only eat a few Sprigs of it and often they cant retain it on their Stomachs yet they crave it. I have found dead grass in lions Stomach and in the Stomach of wolves and cats and foxes and wolves and coyotes when green grass was not to be found. The mountain lion is Very careful to carry their young to dripping cliffs of rocks where diferent Varieties of Vegetation grows and can be found fresh and tender even in drouths or cold weather. It is plain to See that only few [*captive*] animals young or old get this privilege. By being deprived of this Special rotation of food they are deprived of the proper amount of exercise they Should have. They [*captive animals*] Should have a chance to walk for miles in day time or at night. Instead of that they only have a Space of 10 or 15 feet to walk in.

It is a habit of most wild animals that live on meats to eat and lay up a day or So then take a long trip on an empty Stomach. There are few animals that fill up and travel far away and lay up for a day or So at a time. The mountain lion requires fresh air. They like to Sun around large cliffs of rocks when the warmth of the Sun can be felt through low brush and at the Same time one or 2 bounds on the rocks would give them protection from man or other animals. They are great to Slip around and hide and often depend on Slipping around among the rough rocks making greater efforts to hide than to race away at full Speed. This means when they are chased with dogs they usually climb a tree or a high cliff or rocks as Soon as the dog or hounds get close to them Say in Sight or 35 yards or So. I have thought they would tree from one dog or a number of dogs either as

Ben Lilly's Tales

they get Very close to them.

It is Said it is Very hard to get a domestic cat to live on a Steam boat. I have talked with Engineers who tried to raise and Keep pet cats and he Said they would not live long on a boat. They have every Kind of food a cat could call for and yet will not live long. He claimed it was for the want of grass. No doubt he was correct. There is no doubt but what dampness had Something to do with it. The real cause would have to be a combination of troubles for he gets every Variety of food that is on the market exercise fresh air fire Sun protection from the wind and is really a privilege character on the boat and cant live. I would like to Know if one ever lived to be 12 years old on a boat.

I would Say in collecting Specimens for the museum at Washington D.C. that the mountain lion of New Mexico is called Cougar. Known as the American Cougar which is its Scientific name. In collecting wild animals this collector is expected to give the common name. That is what they are called or Known by in the locality it is Killed in. You will get its Scientific name when they notify you that they received it. In the Southern States as far as I Know [*the mountain lion*] is called Pantha [*panther*]. On the Gulf of Mexico I have heard them called Pantara [*pantera, Spanish for panther*]. In Old Mexico or Spanish they are called Leon. In Idaho they are Known as Cougars and I would Say it is the Same animal that roves each Section. I have Killed apearently the Same animal going by different names and I feel Safe to Say it is one Specie only. They have Varied but Very little in measurements from the State of Mississippi to the Continental Davide in the West and in cane brakes on Mississippi River on both Sides from the Arkansas line to the Vermillion Bay or Gulf of Mexico. They are found mostly on the Louisiana Side after passing Vicksburg Miss. They are found on the East Side in Sun flower River botoms. They are getting Very Scarce in the over flow region now. They are Still in the State of Cowheler [*Coahuila*] and Chiwawa [*Chihuahua*] and Sonorah [*Sonora*] Old Mexico.

In the States of Miss. Louisiana and Texas people were Killed by them in the earlier days. A trapper told me he Knew 2 boys one 11 years old and one 14 was chopping wood at the house in the evening late and a Pantha caught the 11 year old boy. The 14 year old boy tried to hit the pantha with his axe and it caught him too. It had them both down when a young man who was in a Stable feeding a horse heard the racket and run out and Killed the pantha with a billet of wood that was made to rive boards with. It was not a Very large pantha. Both boys died that night from wounds made by the pantha. The 2 boys were buried in the Same grave at a place called Hickry [*Hickory*] Grove in Mississippi. This was told to me in 1888. He didnt remember the dates they were Killed in but he lived near there at the time they were Killed.

I could mention many cases where people were Killed by panthas in Miss. and La. Judge Henergan of West Carol [*West Carroll Parish*] Louisiana told me of an Indian man and a white man going out on a deer hunt one Snowy day. Started out at one oclock in the evening hunted a while and Saw no deer. They Separated. The white man went one way and the Indian another. The white man came home in the evening. The Indian failed to come in. Next morning the men went out in Search of the Indian. Took his track where the man left him. That day tracked him a mile or more and Saw where the Indian was following a big buck deer track. They followed the tracks about a half miles and found the Indian dead Stretched out on the ground and there was a Very large panthas track.

The pantha had Killed the buck deer. Turned him over Sucked blood from the deers throat and went back on the deer track about 60 yards and climbed a Very large crooked oak tree that was leaning over the tracks the deer made in the Snow. When the Indian was traveling under the tree the pantha bounded from the leaning tree down on the Indian and the Indian fell on his face full length on the ground and never Seemed to even Kick or Struggle. He was carrying a rifle expecting to Kill a deer. The Indian was roled over and Some blood Sucked from his throat and the big pantha Kept on going the Same direction he was going. This was told to me about 1882 or three by Judge Henegan who lived North of Floyd La. The Indian was Killed in the early Settlers days. If I remember correct it was his [*the judge's*] house they Started out from for the hunt.

I had always thought that it was hunger that caused a pantha to

Ben Lilly's Tales

Kill people and this case would contradict that. We Know they are fond of deer and the pantha had his deer and Killed the Indian and never eat either. Only Sucked a little blood. This would Show it is natural for them to Kill moving objects.

In 1906 I was out at a rail road Station in Southern Louisiana called Unis [*Eunice?*] above Lake Charles. I was Shipping hides to Washington D.C. that I had collected in the overfloes and big Swamps East of Port Arthur. I met a Very old man who was Very deaf and a tanner by trade. His wife Kept a hotel. He Saw my hides and became interested in them and we talked the most of the night. He was an early Settler in Texas and was at that time a real frontier man in Southern Texas and he related at least a half dozen cases where panthas had Killed people in the early days.

He told me of a man wife and two Small children Settled near the thickets. He had built a little house and was clearing land to farm. One Saturday evening he went to a neighbors house for Something. His wife was burning trash and Sweeping up the yard. There was cane and briers close to the house and the fence was between their house and the cane and briers. The lady was busy burning off trash. One of the babys began to cry in the house. She went and tended to it and brought the largest one out in the yard and Set it down on the ground and continued to rake up trash and burn it. In a few minutes the one outside began to cry. She Soon got it quieted and began to rake up trash.

The child gave a real Squall and a pantha grabbed the child and bounded over the fence and into dense thicket it went with the child the Mother right after the pantha and child. The pantha was Soon out of Sight and the child in the house was Screaming So She run back and grabed it up and tried to find the first one with the little babe in her arms. While the little one was Squalling the pantha come again. She run in the house with the child in her hand and barred the door with a large Slab of wood that was made to bar up the door with.

When her husband come She was holding the bar and Scraming for life. He ran back to a neighbors house and borrowed a gun to Kill the pantha with. The pantha come back to the door and was Standing Straight up with front paws on the door. The man was afraid he would Kill his wife if he Shot in that position. The pantha made its escape and went back to the thicket. This man told me the neighbors all got together and gathered up every dog and man they could get. Among them was a man by the name of Pane who had a pack of hounds. They hunted 2 weeks Steady every day and if I remember right it was eleven panthas they Killed and never found one Scrap of clothes that was on the child. This old man was a truthful man and a man with a good memory in that line.

In the Spring of 1886 I was in the Mississippi bottoms on the Little Deer Creak on Ward plantation Skinning a big bear that I had Shot that day. Major Hamberling [*Major Monroe Hamberlin*] was out on a hunt. He went down to Smedes [*Smeades*] Station to get my mail and when he came back he Says Lilly I saw a 6 foot pantha on that gravel train that Just passed. It Sprang off of the bank out of the cane and caught at a negro that was Shoveling gravel on to a flat car. Another negro Saw it coming and hollowed at the negro he was Jumping at and he dodged. The pantha Just did get its paw in his Jumper. The pantha was going with Such Speed it Struck the ground on its Side instead of on its feet. There was 10 men loading that car and all had Shovels in their hands. They beat it down and the conductor Shot it in the head with a pistol.

The day before it attacked him the Same negro that it Jumped at went out in the cane which was Very thick and come back Squalling. The other men all laughed at him and called him pantha. He Said a pantha was after him. At the Same time of the day it attacked the Same man in a crowd of 10 grown negros. Just bounded on the Same one and no doubt would have Killed him had it landed on his neck. The pantha could have Sunk its teeth in his neck and droped him in his tracks. The other negroes Seeing it coming was all Saved him. It being a female and 6 foot long I would Say She was about a year old. This took place about 11 oclock in the day and there was 40 negroes working loading 4 flat cars with gravel. 10 men to the flat. The engine was there the conductor and a few other men. That was the last time I heard of any one being attacked by a pantha in the Mississippi River bottoms. I have Killed Several in that Section Since that time. Some on each Side of the Miss. River.

These things is explained to Show the diferent things the Same tribe of animals will do in diferent localities. I could mention many cases where they Killed grown men and eat them and only left but few of the larger bones of their bodies to even get a trace of what destroyed the man. In most every case they would commence eating on the man or woman as Soon as dead and in Some cases they would Start to carrying them off alive and the one they were carrying would be Screaming and trying to fight them away. The localities that had the trouble with the Pantha was mostly in the Miss. River cane brakes from the Southeast corner of Arkansas along down the West Side of the Miss. river in the wildest portion and on the east Side of the Miss. river in its wild cane brakes up above Sunflower River and its cane brakes and lakes. These cases was Very rare where they Killed people and at this day it is not heard of. In about 1897 the Sharbon [*charbon—anthrax*] Killed many Stock both domestic and wild animals of all Sizes and I noticed they [*the "panthas"*] Seemed to disappear from about that time.

To one who has lived in the Western country with the mountain lion traveling close by and never bothering a Single man yet here in the west they Kill colts calves Sheep goats and occasionally hogs grown horses and cows. Every Kind of animal I have hunted has a little diferent foods that they will live on in diferent localities of the country. I found in their Stomach in the Swamps coon Deer Turkey duck and geese and hogs and calf and colts. I have never heard of a Single man being attacked by the mountain lion or the cougar or Leon in Old Mexico and yet I cant See one bit of difference in any one of them called by the different names.

In the Swampy countries in Miss. and Louisiana localities the early Settlers did not own more than 8 or 10 head of cattle and 2 or 4 horses and a few hogs. In the west there is ranches with 5 to 8 thousand cattle and 50 or 60 brood mares and ranches with thousands of Sheep and goats raised in the mountains. Here you See the mountain lion has all of the domestic animals he needs for food and the wild ones to eat on and no need to bother man Kind. The places where Western people live are opener than where a lion would like to Stay. At the time the people was Killed in the Eastern and Southern States they were comparatively unsettled. There was but few guns to be had and ammunition was Scarce. The wild animals that was left there felt that they were Superior to man. He felt as Safe with man as he would with deer or cattle. The Settler in most cases either had the blood or grease of wild animals on his clothes and no doubt wild meats and tame meats hanging in a Smoke house and hides hanging on the fence. All would help attract a pantha. I Know of Some cases where the pantha would be noticed around at times appearantly picking on meats and bones that was thrown away from the house in the wood.

And later one went in a house in day time and Killed a man that was Sick in bed. The other man was his brother. He was clearing land about 100 yards away from the house. He went to the house as fast as he could when he heard him hollowing. Still had his ax in his hand and as he Slipped in the door the pantha pounced on him and wounded him So bad it got away. Both young men died. That I was told occured in the Swamps on the east Side of the Miss. River north of Vicksburg Miss.

A Suad [*squad?*] of negrow men was working their and 2 white men come in to work from the hilly country. They prefered Staying in a Small house that Stood off a little ways from the big building that the Boss and the negrows Stayed in. One of the negrows told them the panthas would catch them out there and they better Sleep in this big house. In a few days they both were Killed. The men had Seen the panthas Slipping around.

From my experience and what I have heard it is reasonable to think that the cat family will naturally have a fondness for human flesh. I have noticed it when there is a corpse in a house. The cats will commence to be and mew the Same as it would be in dressing a chicken or rabit or fresh fish and they will in Some cases try to eat on a dead person. This is Pet house cats. It is not Safe to let house cats get close to a dead person or it will in Some cases eat on it. The dog will not eat on his masters body. Yet the cat and dog eats the Same food their master lives on when they can get it.

I think the reason mountain lions never bother people in New Mexico is because they have So much food that is easier to get than it would be to catch a man. In other words in New Mexico in the localities I have been hunting the mountain lions would consider it eating at the Second table to eat a man. They would prefer wild game to man Kind. If you could See the amount of domestic animals the Mountain lions Kill and the carcases of deer and take the quality of food the mountain lions Select and live on you could Soon understand why they never attack man as a food. They eat at the first table and man takes his Share of the animals that is left . . . . [*Here the page of the original document was torn and a few lines of text lost.*]

If the tame animals get Very poor they hunt wild animals as they are usually in better Shape especially the Deer. In Some localities they are Very bad on wild turkeys. Once a mountain lion Strikes your ranges you can feel quite Sure you are in danger of loosing a number of your young Stock unless it is Killed. The ranches that has the roughest mountains and the thickest under brush the best grass and fatest cattle is the ones that will have to Keep a close lookout for their distruction. Wild animals as a rule differ in their habits and what they eat and at one Season of the year will drift through localities and only remain there a Short time. For instance a continued Snow Storm would [*page of original torn*] . . . and a drouth would force . . . another direction and in . . . insects flyes and nats . . . in one direction for a few . . . and ranch animals . . . . Wild ones travels until they find natural protection and Suitable food. It Seems to be a gift by nature for them to Know what to do under Such conditions.

3

BEARS OF ARIZONA AND NEW MEXICO

By Ben V. Lilly

Editor's note: Ben Lilly's bear manuscript was in bad shape by the time Frank Dobie acquired it from Harvey Forsythe of Santa Rita, New Mexico. Most of the pages were damaged and many were missing. What survived of the old hunter's essay on bears, presumably written in the 1920s, appears below.

◇ ◇ ◇ ◇ ◇

[*The grizzlies of Arizona and New Mexico*] . . . range of mountains the distance of 6 or 7 miles and not eat or drink a thing. It Seems they are traveling to find a good place to lay up for the winter. The Very Same day I would find another about the Same age and made the Same travels and it would have about a quart of food in its Stomach and would be drinking water. It would be equally as fat as the other. It goes to prove that they Varie a great deal in their habits even in the Same locality. This tribe raises cubs every other year. There is cubs raised every year but different Mothers. Some Mothers bring 3 at a time others 2 at a time and Skip one year. The cubs nurse from birth which is in February . . . .

. . . of animals give. The Mother bear Sets up with cub on each breast. If 3 cubs one Sits in her lap and nurses on the 2 back tits. They have tits along down the Sides the Same as a hog yet they nurse as I mentioned. 2 uses the 2 front tits and one uses the 2 back tits. When there is only 2 they use the 2 breast tits and 1 it uses the breast. [*Both grizzlies and black bears have six teats.*] Their eyes open at 9 days old. [*The eyes of grizzly and black bear cubs open when they are about five weeks old.[40]*] Their Mother Stays Very close to them until they are large enough to travel. Goes out and gets food and back to them and take them with her as Soon as they can travel good which is about 6 months old. If every thing is favorable they get out earlier. There has been quite an interest taken in the bears time to lay up and . . . .

. . . when the other bears of Same Species travel over or inhabit they generally take in a distance of about 65 miles. For instance the bear Started North. He would travel the direction that the other bears was in the habit of using in and Search in Several diferent parts on his way and it could be Said he was drifting North. This trip is usually Started on a full Stomach. They generally Kill a fat cow or young Stock or even a large fat bull. In most cases the best beef on the range. Very Seldom one Kills poor cattle. Often he will eat on this carcas for 2 or three days making a big bed close to the carcas So as to watch it. He leaves this carcas with a full Stomach on his rout in Search of other bear. He has . . . .

. . . [*three cubs from*] 1 Mother Same age will difer in colors. One a dark gray the other a light brown and one would be led [*gray*] color. The cubs of this Species are not a perfect Silver tip while young. To get a typical Silver tip it would have to be Several years old 4 to 6. All of this Species when their fur and hair has passed through a cold winter and is fully matured carrys a light marking [*at*] the end of the hair which is caled Silver tip. With young bears this doesnt Show. To get a beautyful Silver tip the bear Should be about 4 or 6 years old and dark markings on feet and legs and under mouth. The blacker the nicer the Silver tip will Show. It looks like Snow or frost on the bears back when it runs at . . . .

. . . with it this Specie usually make the beds under rocks by digging deep holes 6 8 or 10 feet back under rocks or under trees on a hill Side. They are usually born in February and they will begin to follow about with their Mother in about June. This tribe of Bear lays up in the high mountains during the winter months especially January and February. That depends on what locality they are in and how the food they live on is in that Section that Season. The Size and age of the bear would naturally have Something to do with their habits. All of the bears Stomachs closes up at Some time during the winter month more especially in January in real cold climates. [*Bears quit eating when winter denning time arrives, but their stomachs do not "close up" or otherwise undergo a physical change.*] I have found . . . Stumps and under . . . head and Sides on Some . . . their hips are rubbed they . . . hind feet and bite on a tree . . . reach with their head or . . . where one had met with . . . be chased by the Master bear and . . . Small Spruche or pine about 6 inches in diameter that was used as a rubbing tree by bear. This bear that had been chased by the Master of the range would bite this little tree in two Just as high as he could reach by climbing up it a little higher than his head then run down the rocks and Slant and throw it as far as he could from his mouth. I have Seen other grizleys go through that performance when there were no Signs of other bear being after them. It Seems as they do that to try their Strength. These large males Visits these trees rock or bushes they rub on in making their through trips and have certain places dense rough fallen timber little branches [*of streams*] and Springs where Seldom any thing but them ever goes to Sleep in. I have found as maney as 6 or eight beds that the Same big male bear had used for . . . a Space of about 50 yards . . . these beds or holes in the ground . . . touch each other they . . . foot deep and 6 foot round . . . hole in the ground would . . . as though they use 1 of these . . . April until November they . . . a day or So when passing if it . . . winter or Summer. Summer 1 2 days. Winter months much longer. They are often 10 miles to another bedding place Something of the Same Kind. They travel by there and lay up in day time and travel at night. These old male bear of this Specie travels over a Section of bear country from first of April until first of December Stopping where the best food is for Several days in his trips in Search of bear. And if there is food that Suits them they may Stop at one of those bedding places for 8 or 9 days and then Start out in another Search for bears instead of food. They are generally full and they Start for the places they rub and bite on trees and Small bushes. At Some of these points if Smaller bears or Mother bears are near these travels of his they . . . on the tree or meet the bear . . . cow or fresh beef they . . . go to the food or . . .

this big fellow will . . . the country that he . . . bite off bark. He will look over a . . . and manage to Keep in touch . . . and food in that Section and he will not come back the Same way he goes up. This Species move about Some during the main time for them to lay up in the South western portion of New Mexico.

I was trailing a big grizly bear in April 1913 on the Blue river west of the New Mexico line. 3 days later I Killed him at the head of Whorton [*Horton*] creak in the white mountains of Arizona [*at an elevation of about 9,000 feet*]. I had Shot him 3 times in the Same hip at Very long range running from me. He went to a cave that he had used that winter. This cave was 6 or 8 feet wide and about 16 feet deep. The wall or mouth of this hole Showed that this bear went in and dragged dirt out of this cave at 6 diferent Stages of the Snow during that winter. The Black dirt would Show it was cleaned out on one foot of Snow and it Showed that it had been cleaned 6 times on diferent Snows. He went in this cave and I found lots of blood but . . . He had gone 300 yards to the East lay down . . . Snow in an old Summer bed he had Scratched out. Lay there a while and moved 15 Steps . . . and Scratched out another Summer bed and lay down in it and beds each Showed blood in them and he was Still bleeding from his wounds. The Snow was about waist deep. His track was Very plain and Some was frozen So no tracks was made. I had a Slow track dog tied to me. This was a Very thick mass of Spruc under growth. I heard a Squack in the dead aspen Saplins and was trying to place myself to take a Shot at him going east and he poped out right in front of me. I fired hitting him in the breast center. Stoped him. The next Shot Struck him under the eye. He fell up against my Side. He Seemed to be drawing long breaths. I fired another Shot in for his hart. I was boged up in Snow waist deep and couldnt See his head. I was wearing a Knife 18 inches long. I drove it for the heart. That finished the work. I was 3 days without a mouth ful to eat in deep Snow. I Kept from freezing by making big fire. Had no coat.

I followed a large grizly bear that Killed 2 head of cattle from New Mexico . . . [*to*] Escalder mountains [*Escudilla Mountain in Arizona, elevation 10,900 feet*] and found a cave he . . . made 12 trips in and out during the lay up . . . Season where these 2 Very old grizlys made 18 trips in and out of their caves.

[*It is hard to believe that Lilly could accurately determine how many times a bear left and reentered its den during the winter by casually observing the snow at the den's entrance. One would have to cut a trench in the snow and study its stratigraphy in the manner of an archeologist to assess a bear's movements with such precision. Also, Southwestern bears have been known to leave their winter dens for brief periods before spring, but this isn't a routine behavior, especially in the highest, coldest mountains. For a grizzly to exit and reenter his winter sleeping quarters twelve times, or even six times, during a denning season seems excessive.[41]*]

The first one I mentioned Killing him near the cave made 6 trips in and out during laying up Season. He was the largest I Know of being Killed in the Rockie Mountain district. He was Killed April 3 1913. He measured 9 foot from end of nose to end of tail [*and*] 8 foot around the bodye at Shoulders and reer in front of hips. His hind foot was 12 inches long and 7 inches wide across the pad of foot. The front foot was 7 inches wide across the pad. He was 5 foot 8 inches high [*and*] measured 18 inches around legs where foot Joined the leg. His nails was 5 inches long on front foot and as broad on top Side as a mans nails. This is the largest bear and track I have been able to find. I hunted bear Since 1882. That would lead me to believe that South West New Mexico and Joining portions of Arizona has had the largest bear I have found . . . locality . . . that I have hunted in.

[*Adult male grizzlies in Yellowstone National Park average about six and a half feet from nose to tail with the tape following the contour of their backs. This figure is larger than that obtained with a rigid measuring device.[42] Obviously, Lilly's nine-foot grizzly was a storyteller's invention.*]

I commenced hunting July 4 1912 on the Blue river and . . . Frisco river from Alma N.M. to Alpine Arizona. The cattle men paid me bounty on bear and mountain lions. By the first of January 1913 I Killed 47 bear and lions. In 1913 I Killed 48 bear and lions. There was about equal number of each Variety Killed the 2 Seasons. This I mentioned to Show what a great home it was for bear and lions each. The bear and lions were Killing cattle every day on the diferent ranges. The lions were Killing cows calves and colts horses and Sheep. There is more Variety of food in the South western portion of N.M. and Joining State [*of*] Arizona than I have found in other

States and So many cattle raised and running loos on the wild range and high mountains. There is Pinyons acorns and Several Varieties of Juniper Berries. The high mountains is well watered dense Forest ruged Rockie mountains with dense under growth. A real home for wild . . . . The Bears that was Killed in 1912 and 1913 . . . Grizlys Brown and Black. 2 Varieties in . . . Species.

A little more about the laying up . . . . The Grizly or Silver tip (comonly called) they travel occasionally at all times of the year. I will Say they eat nothing after their Stomach closes up yet they ramble around Some and in Some cases come back to the Same beds and at other times make a long trip across baron ranges traveling to other mts. It happens that Very large bear will have 3 or 4 dens and will go by them before the Snow and fix 2 or 3 beds up a little as he goes by and a Mother bear will fix up Several beds in her travels and you can See places of that Kind that has been used for years by diferent Sized bears. A bear will travel at times and it Just pouring down Snow. I often Say . . . the locality the bear lives in is to rough for a man to travel in. In the early Spring they come down to the warmer grounds and commence eating Vegetation that Sprouts . . . . The Snow melts off and usually find Vegetation . . . around little branches [*creeks*] high up in the mountains . . . . They eat on old carcases that lay frozen . . . the Snow. As Soon as they begin to eat after Some Kind of Vegetation and Some flesh usually deer or carcases of cattle that frozen under the Snow then they go back up the mountain and try to find acorns and Pinions and nuts [*pinyon nuts*] that was covered up by Snow and remained all winter. Bear Know where Such food was and will return to these places to get it. They also can tell about how Soon it can be found from on top of the Snow. The large male bear is the first one to make a Stroll over the territory in Search of food. Then the Bearon Bear male or female 2 years old and up follows behind him. Maybe 12 or 14 days after he is gone the largest one or 2 at a time first then the 2 year olds gradually works that way then the old Female bear and year old past cubs comes. About June along comes the Female and the February cubs Slowly drifts over the ranges. This applies to . . . their habits in a real wild where there . . . plenty for them to live easily on.

Now . . . think that they all Start the Same day . . . get in the big road to travel. They Strike out and feed along over the range looking for anye thing that they like to eat. They have their traveling grounds Selected from manye years experience and ones who have not the experience has the natural instinct. This believe to be true from my association with the bears tracking them up and Studdying their habits. After following a bears track for a mile or So I have the ide of his trip reasoned out whether it is Just prowling or in Search of Some certain food and I can look at the country ahead and can tell where that bear is likely to go Knowing their nature and having the benefit of Seeing what it did while I was tracking it. That I Suppose is the way they Keep out of trouble and the first large bear rubs and bites on the trees and the Smaller one goes to those places. This large male bear Seldom ever comes back the Same way he goes up. I have Seen where the bear used these tree . . . more than 20 years. Every bear will try . . . over a Very large range in a Season and often fatten and go 40 miles to bed up. That is when there is meat or food they Stay to fatten and come back to lay up.

The Black and Brown bear of New Mexico Seems to be the Same Species. In all the ranges I have found them in especially the high mountains they Varie in color from a Jet black to a bright yellow. The Jet black ones will at certain Seasons of the year usually July and August if Very poor and ready to Shed of their winter fur and hair they will turn Brown for a Short time. The new coat of hair and fur will be fine and about grown by the last of November and it will be Jet black if the Bear is in good health and fat and is apt to remain and improve in appearance until about the first of April in an altitude ranging from 9 to 12 thousand ft high.

The Mother of the Jet black bear usually raises from one to 3 cubs. The year She gives birth to young . . . that ocurs only once in two years that is . . . raise one year and Skip one year. The young Mother is not as brave to take care of the cubs as the older Mothers. A few young Mothers of this Species will break off and run away from the cubs when the dogs find them in a bed together and the older ones will fight furiously and See that they get up a tree before She leaves them and will often go up the Same tree and Stay up there with them. If the little cub is caught by man or dogs and it Squalls or cries the Mother breaks for it at once and will attack what ever has caught it. It often ocurs if the cubs are large enough to climb good they [*the mothers*] will Scratch on the tree with their front feet and make a roaring noise. If the cubs runs up a tree She will climb up and Stay up with them and they often get the cubs up and they will run Just as far away as they can go. It look as if they try to get their enemies as far away from the young as possible and will come back . . . the young as Soon as they get rid of the . . . or man that chases their young away. Their method of getting rid of them is to out run and dodge off from them.

The Cubs are Very Small at birth about the Size of a grown rat. Their eyes open at nine days. [*Actually, the cubs' eyes open about five weeks after they are born.*[43]] They are usually born in January or February and the beds the Mothers and cubs Stay in is under rocks or caves that they Scratch out under the ground. Occasionally they carry leaves and Straw in these beds that is dug out by them and the Mother will bring them out in May and June and they will travel Some with her and in Some Sections She will commence feeding them on black Ance that they Scratch out of old rotten logs or under barks from dead trees. Sometimes the cubs Say 3 from the same Mother will be diferent in color. One black one brown and one So light in color it will look yellow at a distance. And I have Seen 2 Jet black cubs with a Brown Mother. Yet it is Safe to Say that there is a Specie of bear in New Mexico black or brown . . . brown Known as black bear and the brown . . . is called brown bear and they are the Same Specie. Both color feed on Same range and Same Kind of food. When cubs is Very Small the Mothers will turn over rocks and get eggs that the black ants lay under rocks and under logs and in dead bark on Stumps. Old bear feed on Some too.

Old ones eats Vegetables and nuts and roots of diferent Kinds [*and*] berries and bugs. They eat nuts and acorns and wild fruits of different Varieties. New Mexico in the South west portion has Very fine ranges for bear and each Variety grows to make fine Specimens. They have a number of high mountain ranges that is well watered and many Varieties of food that is not found in Still higher altitudes. And there is numbers of cow ranches that offer them the choicest of beef to eat and all of the larger Sizes is continuously Killing cattle. Every Variety I Know of Kills cattle if the cattle range in the Section that they Select for their homes. If a bear is 6 years old male or female . . . is Safe to Say they Know what good beef . . . and once they get the taste of it they will . . . and eat the fattest one they can find when hungry. There is cases in N.M. where the bear has caused Ranches to be abandoned on account of the bear Killing the cattle. The grizly first makes his rounds and Kills then the other bears eat at the Second table for a little while and Soon the others make their own Kill. Bear usually Kill cattle in Such a rough place that the cow that is Killed is never found and many persons express themselves as not believeing that bear Kills cattle. No doubt they think they are correct. The Same thing doesnt apply to every locality. The bear is like a man is by Oysters. Once he travels over the Oyster regions and gets a taste of them he will want them as food. And I will Say the bear might have its first beef Killed for him yet it would only be a pleasure to him to Kill his beef and roam the forest for glory as well as to Stave off Starvation. The Bear would even be Satisfied at beef he would get Some how . . . .

[*Just how great a threat black bears pose to range cattle is still debated in the Southwest. Some ranchers in bear country agree with Ben Lilly and insist that cow-killing bears are not rare and that a bear with a fondness for beef can do more damage to a herd than a mountain lion. Biologists and conservationists tend to discount the ranchers' stories of severe bear depredations on cattle.*]

There is a bear in New Mexico that Resembles the Grizley and the Brown and Black bear. This I take to be a diferent Specie from the other Species mentioned. The way it differs from the Black and Brown bear is it has toes webbed together from the pad of the foot to the front of the toes. This webbing is the Same as the webbed foot of a grizley bear has [?]. They also have a Joint in their hind foot the Same as the grizley bear [?]. The grizley Species have web feet from the pad of foot to the front of toes and a Joint in their hind foot. The nails on the Grizleys front foot is long and Slender. A grizleys front foot that would be 7 inches wide. The nail will be 5 inches long on the top Side of the nail. The hind foot 12 inches long 7 inches wide. The back nails is Short on hind foot. The web footed Brown bear I Speak of has front nails Something like the Grizzley and Black bear Species. The bear I mentioned as being diferent resembles the grizley in Some of its . . . make up and also the Brown and Black . . . carries about the Same Size and the colors compares with each

Ben Lilly's Tales

Variety under Some conditions Varying from a Jet black to a light brown to a mahogany color. I Killed a Very large Black male on Gilla [*Gila*] river 20 miles north east of Cliff N.M. He was Very old and was about 6 foot 6 inches long from the end of his nose to the end of his tail. His front foot was 5 inches wide and his hind was nine inches long and 3 inches wide. The length of the foot and width would be about the Same as a grizley or Brown or Black bear of Same length. The main diference Showed plainest in the feet. They are webbed from the pad to the front of the toes. The hind foot also is webbed and has a Joint in the hind foot and a Small Seam in it that is exactly the Same as a grizley or Silver tip. And his nails is formed and proportioned the Same as the black or brown bear. I Killed and found them in North [*New*] Mexico north of Taos N.M. The ones in that Section was a beautiful brown Very dark. This was Small. Killed in November [*1921*]. I Saw 2 other female hides of Same tribe of bears . . . . The form of the feet Seemed to Show the main diference. They traveled and fed on the Same food and Same territory as the Grizley and Brown bear did. The one in the Gilla river Section was a real cow Killer.

[*Two species of bears are native to the southwestern U.S. and northern Mexico—the grizzly and the black bear. Hair color varies considerably within both groups and cannot be used to determine a bear's species with certainty. However, examining the claws on the front feet is a sure way to classify a bear. Grizzlies have long, slightly curved claws on their front paws, much as Lilly described them. The claws on the front feet of black bears are much shorter than a grizzly's and are tightly curved, like those of a cat. Lilly's third kind of bear apparently had black bear claws and thus must have been a member of that species.*[44]]

It is Very Safe to Say that all full grown bear that is raised on large ranches where the cattle Stays in the rough mountains the year round and it is too rough for a man to ride in and is rough enough for a bear to feel Safe from man once they get the taste of fresh beef whether Killed by man or accident you can count on full grown bear Killing your cattle when ever they get real hungry and the cattle tries to live in the Same Section that the bear lives in. The bear of course doesnt Kill cattle in every Section the fatest cattle uses. In a rougher locality than the man rides in if I find a large bear track I can take a big bears track and it is Very Seldom that the bear doesnt Kill or pass a carcas of a cow that he Kills in a distance of 20 miles travel on his trail or travel. This applies to a large locality where there is Several thousand cattle in a wild locality that the bear feels at ease to live in and not be chased or Killed by man. I have followed big bear for twenty miles from one mountain range to another. They would leave a Kill and travel for 10 miles and Kill another cow and not eat one bit of it. Go 10 miles Just to get a real good hiding place. There is but few men who Knows the habits of a real old bear and then too but few men who Keep close account of their losses in rough mountain ranges. There has been Several real good ranches in New Mexico abandoned on acct. of the bear being So bad about Killing and chasing their cattle out of their Very best ranges. New Mexico has localities that grows Some Very fine Specimens of bear where it is not too closely Settled up. There is localities where the food that grows in the . . . .

4

BEN LILLY'S MOUNTAIN LION KILL RECORD FOR 1916

Editor's note: In the summer of 1916 Ben Lilly signed up with the Bureau of Biological Survey as a hunter for the agency's new predator control division.[45] Mountain lions were his specialty, and his hunting territory was southwestern New Mexico and Greenlee County in southeastern Arizona. Program supervisors required the government hunters to keep a record of their kills in diaries. The following account, Lilly's first attempt at keeping a diary, is a discussion of the eight lion kills he made from June to September 1916. Two small kittens were captured alive after their mother was killed, bringing the number of lions he removed from the range to ten. Ben Lilly hunted for the Biological Survey on a part-time basis and was paid for about thirty month's of work before being discharged from the organization in August 1920. Records show he was credited with killing fifty-five mountain lions and twelve bears during this time.[46]

◇ ◇ ◇ ◇ ◇

This Book Sent to me Some time in July and it was Sent out from the Post office about the 15th of July and it was Some time in August before I was abel to get it. For that reason the trailing and Killing of Lions will have to be copied from my memory as the diarys has all been Sent in.

Male Lion No 1
Copied From Memory.
Killed June 14th 1916
40 [*25*] miles North of Clifton Arizona between Sqaw creek and rousing Sat [*Rousensock*] Canion. West Side of Blue river about 4

miles West. This lion had a range of about 35 miles that I trailed him over 4 times. The lower End of the range bordered on Sardine Canion on the South North to the Blue range East to Blue River and west to Eagle Creak. In the 4 trips he went a little diferent. At 3 diferent places he made the Same trips for a distance of 200 yards. 4 trips. One was in a box canion around Some rocks. One about 4 miles North of that in a Short canion leading in to a big canion and a Scup Spring on a rock [?] and the other was 4 miles west. He would pas between large bluffs going North and west. This Seemed to be about the center of his range and the main range for Female lion to lay up during the day. The male lions Visit these places about every 14 days.

Seem to Varie more from feed Stand point than ainye thing else. If they catch a animal they usually if in a dens thicket or good hiding place they eat a bate [*meal*] lay up a day by the carcas and Eat another bait. Then they Strike out hunting up other lions. Their routs is governed Some by the Situation of the other lions as to when thy will go. If the Females and other lions have moved they will try to go to them and then on to another family of lions. On these travels the male will usually mak two Strokes with the front paw in loose Straw or dust under a tree or under a cave [*an overhanging rock?*]. In a dry place usually. All of the Males does this pawing in their Travels where they are looking for other lions when they are Traviling on a full Stomach. The Kitten males that I have had as pets feed them Soon in the morning and he will if led out quietly on a chain will paw in Soft Straw and look a way off as though he wanted to go. This applies to One that is Tame and not Seavege and up as large as a house cat. The half grown wild ones does this pawing a round when they eat a bait and Start To water or den.

[*It is believed that male lions make these pawing marks or "scrapes" to designate their home ranges or territories. A tom's home range may overlap a neighboring male's to some degree, but for the most part an adult male does not share his home range with other males. The scrapes are thought to announce the resident male's presence and serve as "keep out" signs. The scrapes or scratches are sometimes augmented with urine or feces, adding the tom's scent to his marker.*[47]]

Young lions half grown drinks lots of water and old ones Very little. More when they are giving Milk. It is not Safe to Say lions can be located by watering places but a man who under Stands the habits of lions can tell the direction and range thy are using mostly by there pawing places. It is Slow but can be worked out So as To get the general out lines of ones range. The large males usually come back to a carcas to See if other lions has been a round in about 12 days after it has been Killed. The lions that the male Visits will usually go to a carcas that he has eat off of. The female usually leaves her young near a carcas until She catches another then move to it and from that to another they move. Stop catching when they are Suckling. They go out and Kill and bury even Night. They will go 2 days Travel Some Times before coming to thier young if large Size or about weaning time.

I Some Times find where one lion has Killed 3 animals in one night usually a colt or calf and a deer. Some Times 2 deer and a calf. They drag deer and calves off and bury them by covering them with Straw and leaves in hidden places. The colts they dont hide So carefully. The cows fight them and bellow and low a round for their young. The horse Soon leaves and dont Seem to return. The lions is great for making raids. They Seem to drift after other game and at times they Seem to be plenty full then all gone. In July and August they Seem to Turn their attention to fawn Deer and at that Season if one is caught it is only one bait for a lion and he will hunt Some where else for his next bait. The deer does its best to Keep the fawns moved out of the way. So they are Very hard to locate in July and August when deer is plentiful. Especially in August as the fawn can follow the Mother then.

As I have given Some of the habits of lions as I under Stand them I will go a head with the trailing and Killing of 1 as I remember it. On friday before the 14th of June which was on Tuesday I had been working Several days on old traces of the big fellow trying to get tracks that was good enough for the dogs to go on. On Friday they got a track that they could handle. There was 2 the male and a female. The dogs Split up in 2 packs and Some of the dogs Stayed out all night. Saturday was worse trails and nothing Started. I lay over Sunday. Dogs tied up when I quit Saturday night. Monday picked up the Trail. Trailed North and late in the evening [*it*] quit going South. Tuesday I picked up Track early and at 11 oclock we found where he had Killed a calf about 3 months old. There dogs got mutch faster and while I was climbing out of Some cliffs of rock got out of hearing. I hunted all day and failed to find them. At day light Wednesday Morning I heard them South of me and at 9 oclock AM I found them tread up a pine. I Shot the lion and He lodged in the tree. Was So Stiff He didnt fall out. I cut the tree down to get Him. He was a Very old male and had a little of the toes of one front foot off. His Track was Very easily identified. The Measurement and data can be gotten from the [tag on the] hide at the Byological Survey and put in if necessary. S c [stomach contents] calf.

There was 4 calves Killed in a week while I was Trailing Him and a female that was eating on the calves With him. They boath Eat together that week. In bringing the hide out Thursday I Saw the females track going west. The dogs could trail it Some So I Took the hide on and went back friday after the female. Male Lions Never Paw up Straw or leaves when they are traveling to catch Something or feeding. They usually find or hunt fead [?] colts [on] rainy Nights and calves they Seem to follow to one Side crossing from one Side of the tracks to the other. They work deer mostly from front. Way lay them. They often quit one bunch of Stock and go 5 or 6 miles to another and make a catch or Killing there.

Female lion No 2
Copied from Memory.
Killed about June 20 1916
45 [30] miles North of Clifton Arizona
head of Thomas Creak East Side of Red Mountains about June 16. I found track going west. Followed until night. Was going North west. I lost Track. Hunted West Saturday found no Tracks. Lay over all day Sunday. Monday I found Track of Same lion. Trailed East and South. Lay out at night. Took Same track at 6 oclock AM. Trailed until about one oclock and Killed her on head of Thomas Creak. I Saw the dogs Trail up to her. She was laying up in a Small Juniper Tree. Jumped out and ran 400 yards. Treed and Jumped out a gain and made a run. I Shot her running in a little Trail Towards Me. When She Saw me She Stopped a bout 10 ft away and made a low growl Just as I Shot her Standing Still. She didnt Seem Vicious. Was

Just a Surprise to meet me in that way and Seemed to Stop To Study out Something better to do. I fired on her and She fell dead. S C perfectly empty. The Female No 2 had Several Scars on her where She had been bitten by the Male that I Killed No 1. His front teeth has been broken and the Scars Showed the works of the broken teeth.

About 3 years ago I caught a female lion in a Trap and a large Male came a long about the time She had drug the Trap 300 yards and Jumped on her and bit her in Several places. There was Snow on the ground and the tracks and the biten places on her Showed. She was caught in a No 5 bear Trap and a Very light drag. She had 2 yearlings that had been with her. The hounds Took the Trail and I Killed them bouth that Evening late. The next day I Trailed the big he all day and it come a Snow that night. He was 3 days a head of me and it was Entirely Snowed out at night. If I am correct on Tracks Was the Male No 7 that I Killed 23 august 1916. At that time He made only Occasional Visits to my territory.

Female Lion and 2 Kittens Captured alive
No. 3. 4 and 5 Copied from Memory.
About 56 [40] miles North of Clifton Arizona Old She was Killed July 3 1916. 2 Kittens captured Same day. I first found Sighn of the old one South Side of K P Canion and 2 or 3 days located and Killed her North of K P Canion in head of canion that Makes out from the head of Staple [*Steeple*] canion in to K. P. Canion. She was at Foot of Blue range East Point between K P canion and Staple Canion. Struck Trail about 1 oclock PM and Killed her and caught the 2 Kittens a while before dark. She trailed to foot of Blue range and back and was laying with the Kittens under a Small bluff of rocks and She fought off 5 dogs until I got in Sight then brok and run 200 yards and went up a Tree. I Shot her out and run to the rocks and found the 2 Kittens as I thought there was Kittens from the way She fought the dogs. I camped there that night. Skinned her and come out the next day and then Sent them [*the kittens*] down to Mr Tol Caspers [*Toles Cosper's Y Bar Y ranch*] to be cared for. S C calf.

Female Lion No 6
Killed July 15 1916

65 [*40*] Miles North of Clifton Arizona
Near West Bank of Fish hook Creak
Near the Mouth 2 Miles North of Blue River.
I had hunted for 2 days West and North and South and No Tracks to be Seen. I Struck her Track in the evening and Trailed her a little while and in among Some big Bluffs at water the dogs Jumped her. She ran back west and Treed. I Shot her. Found She was Suckling So I hunted the Kittens until dark and Skinned her next morning. I found no Sighn of Kittens. It rained that night and Every day for 4 or 5 days in Shours at diferent Times each day. So I had No Show for Tracking. Only had to hunt by guess. I found her old Tracks in Several directions for 5 or 6 miles a way under rocks but got no Trace of the Kittens. It Seemed from the condition of her Woumb they must have been as large as half grown [*house*] cats. S C Deer.

Male Lion No 7
Killed Augst 23 1916
75 [*45*] Miles North of Clifton Arizona
Near head of Bush Creak West of Big Red Bluffs in big Box and Bluffs in a west Prong of Bush Creak. This Lions Track was found about the 4 or 5 day of Augst. Very old. While I was trailing a female lion his old Sighn was going East up Noling [*Nolan*] canion. It had rained that day and it Seemed to be about 4 days old. At that place there was a buck deer Killed for Several days and the female lion and him had boath been there. The Female I was Trailing was two days a head of Me and it comenced raining at 1 PM and Continued until night. I Stopped there until morning and next day at 3 pm I found the She lions Trail and Kitten Tracks and Trailed them until dark and past. I found where the old he Killed a colt. [*The kill was*] Several days old. I tied the dogs up and at night. 9 oclock it came a rain and at 11 oclock rained again. At day light the dogs could not Start it [*the track*] and it was Very late in the evening before I could find aneye trace of it. It [*the male lion's track*] had rained out So I Trailed her until dark and camped on Track. The next day I worked around and found it a gain but She had left the Kittens Some where. Finally lost her Track. I had had nothing to eat for over 2 days. I come out and eat and fed the dogs.
    Next day I went South on the west Side of Blue river. It come a

Ben Lilly's Tales

rain at 10 am and 2 or 3 more Shours that day. My camp was at Blue Ranger Station. I went down and moved it up and then I found the big lions Track and I followed it until rained out. Followed him off and on until the 23 of Augst. The rains would cause me to lose the dogs and then him. The way I finally adopted a plan to get him I Tied the dogs and turn them loose in Sections one at a time. After each Shour I would turn loose another dog. By doing that I managed to find them after a rain.

The Shour was mutch lighter that day [*August 23*] than had been the day before. His Trail was Started at 6 oclock Am and he was trailed until dark or dusk the Same day. It rained 2 or 3 times. His trail was found at 6 AM going west. He then turned South then up a Slope North crossed 2 canions West then climed a big bluff going North that put him on Top point of Blue range. Then he Struck west and then North. There went in to River Rocks of Cather [*Castle*] Creak then Took a pack trail west for half mile then turned South then back west through open Piney woods then South upon Top of East Slope of Blue range. Then I Saw where 2 horses run a way from him. He followed after them Some distance then went west higher up the davide and got in to a bunch of cattle. They Seemed to be laying down and they Seemed To make fearful lunges getting a way. He followed a Short distance after them then he turned South and Took a bucks tracks and followed them a mile or more to the East Slope and then Went down in a canion and up a davide going South then on Top and West then South. At [*that*] time I heard 2 dogs Trailing that I hadnt Seen Since 6 oclock. It was then about 12 m [*noon*]. They Seemed to be South. My pack went South in to the big canion and down it east and up on the cliff rocks then west to top of Davide. From there they went South and east and down in another big canion and went up it west to point of Blue range. There came a rain. It was Very thick and it Seemed that the lion track got fresher from there although it was raining. During this rain I let another dog loose and things worked well for a while. Thene another rain. They were going South and up a davide. The one that was a head took down a canion for Several miles and at 5 oclock another Shour came and a loss [*of the track*] and late I found the way it went going north and East. It finally got in a old Pack Trail or Road and the dog I had lost it. By this time all [*the dogs*] I had was gone but 2. One Tied to me and one trailing up. So I could See it was getting late and I quit My Trailing dog and commenced running from Point of Mountain to Point listening for the dogs that had been gone So long and 2 or 3 runs put me in hearing. So I got the coarse and ran for life for a mile and as I was nearing the dogs the lion Jumped out [*of his tree*].

They Soon Treed a gain and I Slipped up to a big bluff. Under me was a Very thick Spruche. I was peeping down at Some things hind feet I could See on a limb below me. I Moved a little and down came the lion Swoping down the Tree. I fired on his neck as He went to the ground. Wow wow went the dogs and I Kept a Keene eye on all of the cliffs and rock to See him pop out. Soon they made a temporary Tree Bark. I Kept on the watch until they all Tread good. It was getting dark. I Scrambled down the ledge and Kept fairly well hid. When I Saw the dogs one was barking at the root of a old broken off lodged Stump about 20 ft high that was leaning between 3 thick Spruche. One dog ran up the Stump and looked up a Spruche that Stood 12 feet or more to the north of the Top of the Stump or broken Tree. I Spied his [*the cat's*] head about half way up the Spruche in thick brush. His bodeye was hid. I fired on his neck and down he came. The dogs chewed him Some and He Seemed to be abel to bite although he was badly wounded. I Stabbed him with a Knife in the heart. My first and last Shot hit the Same place on the neck though first one making only a deep flesh wound.

I rolled his entrels out and hung him up the best I could and blundered off in the dark for water and found a Spruche Tree that Kept me fairly dry the night. I fed the dogs on lion. I didnt have nothing to eat as I had been 2 days finding the Trail and one day on it. I went in a cave the night before and found a Big rattle Snake. I Killed him and Told him he might have company. So I Took the rain in preference of a chance of a rattler. Next morning I was roasting Some ribs of the lion for the dogs So I got to taisting it and I thought I would eat 1/4 of the lion before I got enough. He was old poor and tough to. He had had one front leg injured at Some Time and I could tell his track when I would See it. He had been passing through that country for over 2 years. Come in first from frisco River the East Side. Would come through once or twice a year and for the last 12 month or more this was his principal home from Alpine to Blue Po [*post office*] South in arizona a distance of about 20 miles and from the Blue range West to the east of the Frisco. I had trailed him Several diferent times. Once a big Snow Saved him and 2 other times rains. Once I Killed 4 [?] and had a Very old cold trail and that night it come a light Snow and put out the track. He Killed 4 colts in august besides deer and calves that I Saw and I am told that he Killed one thousand dollars worth of Stock this year Since January last. Several 2 year old horses was Killed South of Alpine. The loss was heavye on Colts from what the people tells me and Perrys horse ranch lost heavy and on East Side of Blue Nolan and Johnson canion. I asked the neighbors and Stock men to make out a list of what they Knew to be Killed by the lions and have it Sent in to the Byological Survey or notify Mr Ligon Predatory animal Inspector at Albuquerque N.M. The Rains was bad and Success Seemed out of the question in Killing him on act. of Continnuous Shours. 5 or 6 men promised Me that they would Make out a Statement of Just what they had lost by lions but failed to do So. I felt like I was Staying Two long on one animal but He was there and it was my business to Kill the one that was doing the most harm. The inspector [*J. S. Ligon*] told me not to Stay to long after one old hard lion [*but*] to go where they were thick. It Seems he Knew my weak Point is to Stay with an animal regardless of resistance. We can Say that He is out of the way. S C Fawn Deer.

Male Lion No 8
Killed Sept. 12 1916
160 [*100*] Miles West of Sacora [*Socorro*] N.M.
on Frisco River 6 Miles East of Luna and on West Side of river 3 miles west of Dillion Mts [*Dillon Mountain*]. I worked at this lion about 7 days. Mr Laney Had a colt Killed about 2 weeks [*before*] in his pasture and I camped near there and hunted through the Pasture and no tracks. It was raining Every day or So. Not even old Sighn could be found. I then took a Small pack on my back and went South and west. Had 3 rains that day. I Saw where a bob cat had Killed a fawn deer. I laid out under Tree. Rained twice during the Night. The next morning I found old lion Sighn going east and west. I took the East end. It was 4 or 5 weeks old and at 4 oclock I had worked it east and across frisco river in the head of the big box. That evening late I found Sighn the dogs could Trail So we worked it up deavils creak

Mountain Lion Kill Record

[*Devil Canyon*]. It Seemed to be about 2 days old and was rained out except under cliffs or rocks in the canions. A little before dark it rained heaveye for a few minutes and no Stars was Seen before 1 oclock that night. Drizzled rain next morning. I got up and hunted east and at 9 oclock Am I found old Sighn going east on lost Springs davide Near the lost Spring Corall. I Knew the Track I Saw the evening before was fresher than that So I worked West and at 11 oclock AM I Sat down to Eat a Tea cup full of rice and davide with 4 dogs. As I began to open the can I happened to think It was Sunday. I counted up and it was. So I Says here goes for a Starve. I never Trail on Sunday. So I moved down under a big pine and Slept for 3 hours. Then I fixed Some bark over a log for a Shead and Spent the night.

Next day we hunted all day with out a mouthful. I found the lion I was after had headed for the Laney Pasture where the colts was Killed. I worked him close to camp and went by and filled up and filled the dogs. Next Morning I was out bright and early. Struck Trail and Trailed 2 lions the Male I Killed and a larger Male. I Trailed them from early in the Morning until 3 oclock and one of the dogs that got off by him Self Treed and Me and My pack that was after the larger Male all went to him and when we got in Sight 2 of the cow boys was waving their hats for Me to come where they were. They had no gun but went to the dogs. They Knew I was coming. I Killed Him. It took an hour or more to get him down the mountain over the rocks. So we Took the lion to Lanies Ranch about 2 miles and I partly Skinned it that night and got up at 2 oclock that night and finished it up by day light. I went back and the dogs Trailed the Same lion to the Tree where he was Killed out of. The big lion Track was a day older than this one and they boath Stayed in the Same range. The big one left the country. I fixed the hide up and Sent it out to Mail and I moved over to Ligo [*Largo*] Canion on Read Deens [*Reed Dean's*] ranch (a Vacant place) Coopers old ranch. S C Colt.

Reed Deens range
Female Lion No 9
Killed Sept 23 1916 158 [*100*] Miles West of Secora [*Socorro*] N.M. This lions track was found on the Ligo [*Largo Canyon*]

Ben Lilly's Tales

Tuesday Morning and I trailed it all day and finally lost it. It was rained on Monday and Made on Sunday before. I found where She had Killed a deer. While I was Trailing her I worked the Mountains from Apacheye davide to Deavils Creak and from lost Springs [*Canyon*] to Tuleot [*Toriette*] lake. I camped on Deavils Creak on friday night and Saturday morning I Struck the trail at 6 oclock and Trailed until 12 AM and Jumped her and Killed her. She was up in a tree in a pillion [*pinyon*] Setting for deer on the davide between lost Spring Canion and Ligo canion about 3 miles South west of the old Cooper Ranch on ligo canion.

She Slipped out of the Pinyon Tree and ran a half mile and Jumped out as I came up. I Shot her and wounded in one Shoulder as She bounded out. She ran about a quarter of a mile and the dogs beyed her on the ground. I Saw claw marks where She Tried to climb a gain but failed to get up. I guess the dogs would pull her back. A bear can clumb with one Shoulder broke. She was Very poor. She Seemed to have raised Kittens. One tit was larger than the others. She must have raised a big family by being poor and the 1 larger tit would one raised Some Times [?]. It could be any one Sucked the year before.

I had a Trail of a Small lion 2/3 grown last friday night the 29 [*of September*]. It was west of where I Started her about 2 miles. One man told me that he Saw Tracks of 4 in one bunch last June 4 miles West of where I was Trailing this one all about one Size that Proberly could have been this She and 3 young ones. Another man Said he Saw where 4 had traveled in the Snow last Spring on the frisco [*San Francisco*] mts. South of the Dillon Mountains. I Trailed the Small one friday night until dark. Tied up and at 9 oclock it rained. I hunted all day Saturday in the direction it was headed but it rained next morning at half past Seven and at 10. You See I could have worked over the Trail and not been abel to have picked up the Track. I was Shure of that lion if the rain hadnt Come. I guess I would have got it. Being a Small lion it might have Turned back in the Same Section it came from. I was going to work it Monday but I had to Send the report off and Ship the hides. The Female No. 9 S.C. perfectly empty.

Mountain Lion Kill Record

No 10 Male Lion
Killed Sept. 26 1916 156 [*miles, actually about 100 miles*] West of Sacora [*Socorro*] N.M. I found old Sighn of this lion on Monday Evening in lost Spring Canions South of circle [*ranch?*] about 2 miles. I then worked South down the rough canions and hill to Frisco [*San Francisco River?*]. Stayed all night at Bill Lewises and Early next morning I eat a lunch and Struck out for the Bluffs and cliffs. At the west end of the first bluff found Track and Trailed from 6 oclock until 10 oclock. They first went north then east and back to the Bluffs under them then back on Top and went North then East and back South then east in to another big canion and back west to north end of Bluffs. There the Track got mutch fresher as though it was a day later than the Track they were Trailing. They Trailed Very fast under the bluff going West. I worked on Top. They finally come out on Top at west end of bluffs and went north over almost the Same routs they had been Trailing on. They Seemed to go up frisco River and back down on the far Side of the River. I was Still on this Side of the river on a high Bluff. I Saw the dogs working Very fast and they were Trailing in to Some Very bad bluffs and Shelves So I Turned a dog loose that I had to listen for me. I felt the lion had no Show to get a way and he would be Shure to be in those rough cliffs. About the Time My Dog got half way I heard them Jump and I Saw the lion coming back down the cliffs and rocks bounding from rock to rock. He came over my Way Crossed the river on my Side and Tread up a Medium Sized pine. It was about 40 foot high and he went half way up. Stood with hind feet on one limb and front feet above on another. A lion will usually make him Self Very Comfortable in a Tree Set down on a limb and rather hide but this one was pleased to be up. He was Stuck up with Porquepine Quills and had Some porquepine meat a foot and hair of the Porquepine in his Stomache. S.C. Porcupine.

Number of Lion Tracks Seen on the Hunt from 35 miles north of Clifton Arizona to Alpine Arizona I would guess a distance of 50 miles air line or 60 miles as a guess through the way it was hunted as about 90 miles and from Eagle Creek to Blue river on South East and West. Blue River on the East and Eagle Creek on the West. South from Sardin [*Sardine*] Canion on the South to Alpine Arizona

Ben Lilly's Tales

on the north.

1 large male Lion Track was Trailed from Thomas creak North to oak creak and lost.

1 old Female Track Found South of Blue Fire look out going towards Rasberry [*Raspberry*] Canion. It was to old for dogs to handle. It had been Rained on. There was bear traps Setting in that Section by Mr. Caspers [*rancher Toles Cosper*]. They [*the ranch people*] told me they would throw [*spring*] them but failed to do So and it was not Safe to work the dogs Where the Traps was.

I Saw where 2 Females had faught over a deer near the mouth of Grant Creak and I Killed 2 Females on the West Side of Blue the one that had 2 Kittens and the one that was Suckling and that is all the Same Lion range and these Tracks was old enough to have been the 2 females that was at the deer fighting. There had been a rain on it and the Sighn was 3 weeks old.

I Struck a Female Lions Track on West Peablo [*Pueblo*] creak and found where it was eating on a calf the lions had Killed. I Trailed Her the bigest part of 2 days. She went over to the head of Blue [*River*] about 10 miles to where She had a Kitten. The rains caused me to loose them. I dont Know wheather She had one or 2 Kittens. It was late in the evening and a bad place to See Tracks. So I will Say one. I Know there was one and dont Know that there was more than one. 1 Female. 1 Kitten. Two lions left in that Section.

I Trailed a Medium Sized Male lion one Evening up Feburn [*Frieborn*] Canion on the East Side of Blue River (12 Miles South of Luna N.M.) until dark. Camped on the Trail. Trailed North the next day and east. 2 rains fell one at 11 AM and a Shour at one oclock. I Worked it back west to the Blue and then North. It was lost 4 miles North of Feburn canion going east. 1 Male in that Section. 1 lion left in that Section.

This is all of the Tracks I Saw Brought for ward From Sardine canion 30 miles North of Clifton arizona to Al Pine Arizona Eagle Creak on the West and Blue River on the East and from Blue Post office North. I went to Peablo Mts. or to the Frisco davide East and Blue range west. 2 Males one Medium Size and a large full grown one. 2 Females full grown. 1 Kitten from track about Size of a house cat. 5 Lions in that Section.

One large Male Lion in Laneys and Reed Deens range using

from 6 Miles East of Luna New Mexico to Ligo [*Largo*] Canion east and to Apachie Mountains North and to Reserve and Luna Trail South. His front Track is Scant 3 inches wide. 2 7/8 of an inch wide is a large Track for this Section. He Kills lots of colts. Seems to be a horse Killer. The old Males is the worst after colts. I Trailed a young lion last Friday about Two thirds grown. Camped on its Track in the Dillon Mountains. Come a rain and put out the Track. Two thirds grown. Two lions in this Section.

7 Lions unkilled. That maneye Tracks Seen Since the 6 day of June 1916 that I Know I didnt Kill.

3 Males 2 larg one medium
2 Full grown Females
1 two thirds Grown
1 Kitten about Size of house cat
7 Lions Still on the range.

Ten Killed

4 males 2 Very old males 1 2 year old and 1 yearling
4 Females all full grown and had raised young
2 Kittens Captured alive 1 male 1 Female

It has rained a little almost every day from the 15 of July until the 5 of September in the mountains where I was hunting and it was Very dificult to Even find a Lions Track whitch could only be found under rocks and bluffs. So I might lead you to under Estimate the amount of lions on that range. This makes one hundred and nine I have Killed out of a part of that Section So they cant be Very maneye unless they come in from other Sections. I once hunted a month South of Alpine Arizona. 6 weeks and never Struck a lion Track in the rainy Season. From the 28 of June until the last of Augst I Killed 2 bear but no lions. I come back in Oct. and Killed 9 lions and 3 bear in 6 days. 3 old She lions and Six young ones. 1 old She bear and 2 yearling. Another year I hunted July and August in the alma Section Near Alma N.M. and up to the 25 of August I only Trailed three lions and the 3 Trails was rained Out. The weather broke on the 26 and the 28 day of Agust I Killed an old She and on the 6 day of Sept. an old he and in Oct. I was at the head of Blue the Same year and Killed 7 lions and 5 bear in Oct.

In Mountain Sections game moves from range to range according to Mast Cold and disturbance of diferent Kinds. Either lions or Bear have [*more*] than one home. At Times they move a way and at other times they come back. They bouth Travel over a large Section of country at Some time during the year. The lion is not Very wild. He will hide most anye where it is comfortable for him. The bear wants cover. A dark dense place to hide in. The bears Stomach rules him. He will go where the best fead is and then to cover to lay up. The lion Tries to Shun the cold in Snoweye times by hunting the South Sides to lay up.

If there is aneye thing that I can tell you about the animals or the country that I am Familiar with I will Cherfully answer Such questions that you would like to have my Opinions on. One thing is Shure. Lions is usually Supposed to be More plentyful than they are. One lion goes over lots of country and Kills lots of Stuff. They dont bunch like other animals. To find [*food*] they Schatter out. One to its Self they Sneak on their prey and work alone while hunting. Other animals will Travel togathr in going to a carcas or moving from one range to another. Usually full grown lions feads to its Self. Kills and hides its prey and goes and hunts its mates after a Killing and they will go back to the animal Killed Together. [*Contemporary researchers state that female lions without small kittens will feed with their subadult offspring, but fully adult mountain lions never gather at a carcass and devour it as a group.*[48]]

There is a Small Black Nat that usis in the High Mountains in July and August that causes the Lions to move their ranges. They are in certain Sections for weeks at a time. The deer and dogs will run to get out of their way and they Seem to go every where in the Brush under Bluffs and in the opening and usually fly from 10 oclock AM until 3 in the evening.

I think the Damage of a full grown Lion per year is about $800.00 with the Present price of Stock in this Section. Yearling Cattle at $35 00/100 and will horses will bred at about the Same [?]. And they usually Kill the Choice animals. The deer is also a consideration of 2 a Week. Out of 109 lions I have found in their

Stomaches one Time Porcupine 12 times Skunk. Deers Horses Cows Sheep goats and in one instance I thought one had Hog in its Stomach.

Experience from
B. V. Lilly
From Green Le [*Greenlee*] county Arizona and Sagora [*Socorro*] County New Mexico. From head of Frisco River to Mouth of Blue River and to head of Blue River East and West. [*Lilly's hunting locales near Alma and Reserve in western New Mexico were in Socorro County prior to 1921. That year the state legislature created Catron County by splitting off the western half of Socorro County.*]

5

BEN LILLY'S IDAHO HUNTING DIARY, 1922

Editor's note: Early in 1921 William Hartman "Bill" McFadden, executive vice president of the Marland Oil Company headquartered in Ponca City, Oklahoma, set in motion the most grandiose hunting expedition North America has seen in the twentieth century. The hunting grounds were to be the Rocky Mountains, from the Mexican border to Canada. The main object of the two-year, moveable hunt was to get McFadden a grizzly bear for his trophy room. But black bears and mountain lions were also on the menu, and the gregarious and generous oil magnate wanted his numerous guests to bag as many as they desired. McFadden assigned sportsman and Marland employee Monroe H. Goode the task of arranging the great New World safari.

In the spring of 1921 McFadden's crew assembled in southwestern New Mexico. Monroe Goode had spared no expense in organizing the affair and had hired a small army of men—horse wranglers, hunting guides, cooks, and camp helpers of all kinds—to insure the comfort and success of the visiting sportsmen. Ben Lilly was one of several hound men charged with finding game for the dudes. At age sixty-four he could still hold his own with the younger hunters. Monroe Goode did not participate in the hunt and placed Colorado outfitter Scott Teague in overall command of the campaign.[49]

As the summer wore on the gang moved to the mountains near Taos, just south of the Colorado line. Here Lilly found the tracks of a large grizzly. As the story goes, he spent weeks trying to corral the huge animal, which was constantly on the move. Ben followed the bear's spoor north into Colorado and back into New Mexico. But he never caught a glimpse of his quarry before winter put a stop to their game of hide-and-seek.[50]

The grand hunt didn't end with the winter snows, it was just put on hold. While the grizzlies slept in their dens, McFadden sailed to Europe, and Lilly, at McFadden's request and expense (reportedly $1,500), posed for a full-length portrait in the Taos studio of the celebrated artist W. Herbert Dunton. As did most people who came to know Ben, McFadden liked the picturesque old hound man immensely, and the two kept in touch by letter long after their hunt was over.

The spring of 1922 found the McFadden party in Idaho. The following autumn, after six months in the Idaho wilderness, the outfit disbanded. What must be the longest-running bear hunt of all time was over. And, although McFadden (who only occasionally visited the hunting camps he financed) never bagged a grizzly, he seemed pleased with the show he put on.

Lilly kept a daily diary during the summer and fall he spent in the mountains of Idaho's Boise and Payette national forests. He later presented the journal to the expedition's patron. In 1940 Frank Dobie obtained a typescript of the document from McFadden, who had left Oklahoma and was living in Fort Worth.

McFadden was absent from the hunting grounds most of the time, and Lilly seems to have kept the diary to provide his truant boss with a day-by-day account of the happenings in the field. Even so, exactly what is going on is hard to determine. Lilly's main objective seems to have been to locate a grizzly and then summon McFadden from his home in Ponca City to Idaho to bring "Old Ephraim" to justice. And if McFadden didn't arrive in time, Ben was prepared to assassinate the coveted trophy for him. Although Lilly found some grizzly sign and a dead grizzly (poisoned), he never cornered a live one. The affair had the flavor of a Keystone Kops caper, and the bears clearly had the upper hand. But no matter how crazy and confused the circumstances, Ben Lilly was always happy if he and his dogs were in bear country.

◇ ◇ ◇ ◇ ◇

Saturday May 27 1922 Banks Idaho
Hunted bear north west of Station. Found trail of a year old male bear late in evening going north east. Trailed until dark going north.

Came back that night. Track was four days old and 6 miles up river from Banks. I wanted to hunt Monday but had to move.

Sunday May 28th
Lay over in camp at Banks.

Monday 29th
Moved to Garden Valley.

Tuesday 30th
Lay over in Garden Valley.

Wednesday 31st
Moved to Lightning Creak [*a tributary of the Middle Fork of the Payette River*]. Struck camp at 4 oclock P.M. I Struck out for bear tracks. I found track of a 2 year old male bear about 3 days old. I got back that night.

Lightning Creak Camp June 1st 1922 near Garden Valley

June 1st Thursday
I was anxious to take a few of the dogs and trail that bear up this morning but Joe and Dr. Myers wanted to work on camp. I went out hunted up Lightning [*Creek*] and found female track and a yearling bears track and found [*the male bear's*] track and worked it back to where I found it the evening before. Saw another yearling bears track during the day coming farther north. I came back to camp at the creak. Joe Doc the packer and Slim had a nice camp fixed up. Dog tent and every thing in nice Shape.

June 2nd
Doc Joe Slim and I took about 8 of your [*McFadden's*] dogs and Crook [*one of Lilly's dogs*] and went up a trail up the east and north Side of Lightning Creak. When we came to the place where I had left the yearling bears track Crook Slipped off and opened up on it while I was under the hill looking for it. Joe Saw it. Was a Very old track and [*he*] Stopped Crook. So we Started down the hill north and down low we found a Small bear track but it was too old to follow.

Idaho Hunting Diary

We then went down the creak. Very rough and Steep. We climbed another Steep hill and Joe missed his gun. I went back and found it for him and met them at another place So they decided to go back to camp and I footed it back through the mountains. They took my horse back. I found where a female bear crossed the river [*Middle Fork of the Payette River*] on a log.

[*Crook was one of Ben Lilly's favorite hounds. When Crook died, Lilly buried him in the mountains north of Silver City, New Mexico, near a shallow cave he used as a semipermanent camp. After Lilly's death, rancher Jack Hooker retrieved the lid of a shoe box from Crook's grave site. On it was written in pencil, "Here lies Crook a bear and lion dog that helped Kill 210 bear and 426 lion Since 1914. Owned by B. V. Lilly. He died here the first Tuesday night in February 1925. He was owned and raised in camp and died in camp here. B. V. Lilly February 1925."*[51]]

Saturday June 3rd
I hunted across the river the way the track was going that I found the evening before. I Struck track of a medium Sized bear. Fairly fresh. I went back and Joe Slim Doc and I went back. Doc Stopped at the river. We went over. Bad crossing Very Swift and we Soon reached the place about two hundred yards from the track. We Stopped the dogs. I went up with Crook Monk and Rambler. Took the track and pulled out. There come Ranger and Lilly [*dog*] Cliff and Several others. There was 8 or 9 all gone right and opening loud and fast. The last two dogs took a cut off and got on the back track that pulled all of yours to the left. They did fine but I Knew they were on the back track. Joe couldnt believe I was right. The dogs run out to where the bear Started from then bayed a porcupine. Some continued trailing on the bear track. Scattered in different directions.

We all davided the best we could and Dr. Myers came across to try to locate the missing dogs that was out. Joe and I found two Airedales that had Just Killed the porcupine. The packer and the game warden had got back to camp and was Shooting a pistol at a target and that was what confused the dogs. Joe and I gathered up what we could find and Doc and Slim picked up a few. I heard Ranger bark last. He was a half mile away barking at the porcupine. Joe heard Doctor Myers Rambler dog trailing and thought it was

Ben Lilly's Tales

Ranger. All of the party got back that night with Several dogs out and Some come in with porcupine quills in them. Ranger failed to come in. I really thought Joe was right when he Said Ranger was trailing. I Knew I heard him at the porcupine make a bark and I was hopeful that he treed. My dogs was out of hearing.

Sunday June 4th 1922
Lay over all day in camp. We picked out porcupine quills as they come in. Only about four got quills in them.

Monday June 5 1922
I took two of my dogs Monk and Crook and tried to find Ranger and they got on a bear trail and trailed it South and a coyote got after them and they had a fight and Kept on trailing the bear. I then found Some coyote pups under a big rock. I came back in another direction to camp. I blew my horn continuously but did not hear of Ranger or See his tracks. I got in late and found the bear we had been chasing had crossed back on the north Side of the river.

Tuesday June 6 1922
Doc and I carried a Spade and ax and tried to dig the coyotes out but they were So Sheltered we could not get them. We dug for two hours and failed to get them. I Struck out to hunt Ranger and Doc and Joe came back to camp. I circled for miles and in the evening I found where Rangers track was right close to the porcupine and the bears track was there. He was following the bears track and came to where the Airedales were Killing the porcupine and I could not See any more Signs of him. I Saw where the dogs Killed the porcupine. They dragged him over four or five different logs and he Stuck quills in logs chunks and every thing. It was a Very large one the largest I ever Saw. I hunted down that canion to the river fully a mile thinking he might be blinded and couldnt travel. I found no trace in that direction So I went in to camp. Got in late.

Wednesday June 7th
I hunted up Lightning Creak on east Side. I found a 2 year old female bear track going north. I came back to camp for Joe and the dogs. Joe couldnt go and Doc took four dogs Cricket and another

Idaho Hunting Diary

Airedale and two hounds. We trailed it until three oclock in the evening. Going north we took the dogs off of the track and Joe and Doc could come next morning and bring the dogs as it was a good place to ride in.

[Thursday, June 8th]
I was up before day and Joe decided they had to move and didnt want to go So I went on with three dogs of mine and in two hours I had three bears a going. One male four years one three year old male a 2 year old female. The dogs tried for a while and then took the big ones track and went off after it. They put one across the river. I caught Crook up and came back after Joe and the dogs. Joe Said he wouldnt risk losing the dogs and asked me to Stay and help cut a tree for a footlog. I did So and they didnt move until next day and decided to Swim the dogs across the river. [*While male bears generally make larger tracks than females of the same age, experts state that there is no sure way to distinguish between the tracks of an immature male and those of an older female.*[52]]

Thursday June 8th [*Friday, June 9th*]
I Stayed in camp until twelve oclock. The men were packing up to move that day. It rained at 12 and the program was to move next morning. I prowled around in the evening looking over the tracks I ran the day before and finally found out where each one went and came back to camp that night.

Friday June 9th [*Saturday, June 10th*]
Packed up and moved over across the river. Crossed Lightning Creak and Payette River and camped at Ranger Station pasture.

Saturday June 10th [*Sunday, June 11th*]
Moved up to Peace Valley.

Sunday June 11th [*Monday, June 12th*]
Sunday we thought it was Monday and I hunted up Peace Valley Creak and east and north. [*Peace Creek is a small tributary of Silver Creek, itself a tributary of the Middle Fork of the Payette River.*] I found 4 bear tracks. 1 male 1 female 1 yearling 1 cub. Four tracks

Ben Lilly's Tales

found during the day. [*Apparently Ben stayed in camp on this Monday to make up for his error in hunting on Sunday.*]

Tuesday June 12th [*13th*]
Hunted east Struck cold trail going east. Joe Slim and Doc took dogs going South of the mountain. Crook Struck running trail of a male bear going northwest. We turned Several of the dogs loose and they all broke a way. It Soon davided down to about 4 Lilly and one of the trig [*Trigg*] dogs [*a strain of foxhound*]. Crook and Lilly give continuous mouth and Dr. Myers Rambler dog was a way behind. They finally got out of hearing going west. It rained that evening. Dr. Myers tried hard to find them. Joe and I were together for Some time. They finally got out of hearing. Lilly Crook Cliff and one of the trig dogs come in next morning about daylight. Crook was Very hoarse. Guess they treed or bayed or they would not have been hoarse. The light rain Kind of put out the tracks.

Wednesday June 13 [*14*]
Rained all day light. I was out Searching for bear tracks and Searching for bear locations. I found no tracks but planned out a hunt for the next day. The men all made a real nice camp at Peace Valley and the dogs have been well fed and every thing Kept in good Shape. Joe is devoted to the care of the dogs. In fact he thinks too much of them to use them. He has lost Six altogether. Ranger was Killed by the porcupine. He was found by Some of the neighbors. Said my tracks were in 40 yards of where they found him. He had quills in his eyes and head and mouth. They pulled them out and tried to lead him out and he fell over dead. It was raining and their dog Kept running out after Something and they went to See what it was and it was Ranger. Five young dogs died from distemper. 2 red ones Coal and Bird dog [*Birdsong hound, a strain of foxhound?*] and one Airedale. I think a porcupine Killed him. We certainly hated to lose Ranger.

Thursday June 14th [*15th*]
Dock Joe and Slim took part of your dogs and I went afoot up on South Side of Peace Valley Creak then crossed over South Fork. Took up high mountain going east. Struck female bear track going

Idaho Hunting Diary

east in mountains on South Side of Peace Valley Creak. Dogs trailed east then north back towards Silver Creak davide. We made a pass at three oclock and finally Straightened it out and we were Six miles from camp and I Suggested we come back next morning going into a country where I thought they would Jump it.

Friday June 15 [*16*]
I was up early and put out afoot. Doc Joe and Slim came along and brought the raw bunch of young dogs. Just a few broke dogs. Joe Said he felt like we wouldnt Start a bear and he would give them Some exercise. My dogs Struck a trail as Soon as I got back up. When I tied them up and when the men and dogs came I Straightened out the trail and took Crook and Monk and held them and gave them time for all of yours and Docs to get in. We turned Crook and Monk loose first. They turned right out. Then we turned about eight of yours loose. They Struck out and away they all went east and uphill. In a few minutes there were dogs running every which way. I had Frank [*dog*] tied to me. I put him on the bears track and followed it. Soon I got in hearing and I heard them baying at a long distance. There were three or four dogs running and trailing in different places. Crook and one of your dogs were baying. I ran about a half mile and your dog Stopped barking. I heard Crook and Monk running the bear. I Saw it about 500 yards away in timber on hillside. Monk and Crook were about 50 yards behind it. I fired Several Shots at it. Cricket was with me. When I commenced to Shoot She put right in after it. She was full 400 yards from it.

I ran over to where I had Shot at it and I Saw one of your dogs come up to where I first Shot at it. He barked both ways on the track but I never Saw him pass. When the bear went the McMullen dog come out and he was Sick and didnt run ten Steps. Docks old . . . came along after I got over there and was looking for blood. I put right in behind and I found blood in Several places. He Soon crossed the trail I went up. I cut a few Small bushes and threw them in the trail. The men or dogs they had with them never found the tracks or blood. I followed them. I found blood that was coming from three places. On left front arm about Six inches from his foot and under his breast as he walked over bushes and on his right Side. He Stayed in water most all evening. I trailed him until night and finally got doubled up when he went two or three times in Same place.

Saturday June 16 [*17*]
I went back up there and took Same old track. Crook and Monk wouldnt work on the track. They Knew where the bear had gone and they would raise up their heads and Start across the woods where they Knew the bear had passed. It took me until 12 oclock to work it out. The bear had been through there the day before I had Shot it and I had that to contend with. I worked the track all of the evening with Frank Crook and Monk. Would cut across and try to go the way they Saw the bear last and not pay any attention to the track. I quit the track late in the evening going northwest making for another range. I circled in every direction and failed to pick the track up. The last time I Saw his tracks the dogs was on it and it was headed for across Silver Creak. He Stopped and traveled in branches or ponds of water from the time he was Shot until night.

Sunday June 17 [*18*]
Lay over in Peace Valley camp.

Monday June 18 [*19*]
There was a man Mr. Heller who Said that there was a bear wallow that the bear used and it was a great place there for bears and as this bear was headed that way and they lay in water when wounded I thought it a good plan to go to it and make a general Search for this bear. Mr. Heller failed to find the wallow. I found three old tracks of other bear. 1 old She 1 2 year old female and a yearling. We trailed and worked across the country until evening. Doc Joe and Mr. Heller went back to camp and hunted back down Silver Creak to camp. Found no trace of the wounded bear. I got back to camp that evening.

Tuesday June 19 [*20*]
Hellers Son and I went back up the mountains in another direction putting in farther South and working higher up. I found tracks of 2 male 1 3 year old and 1 2 year old and a year old female bear track. We found the wallow. It was nothing at all Just a place where little cubs and yearlings occasionally come. We came in that night.

Wednesday June 19 [*21*]

I gathered up Some bear traps and Started up where I Saw the 2 male bear tracks and the females the day before. I got two miles away from camp and I was leading the horse and had my four dogs walking behind. I Saw them raise their heads and make a break. I dashed in before them to Stop them and got Crook Stopped. The others dashed in around me and took the back track. I tied Crook to Maud and Struck out to camp for Joe and the other dog. Joe Said the horses was not up and Doc Myers was out fishing and he wouldnt try to go. Some of the dogs was Sick. It was a male bears track 4 inches wide and 8 inches long and was made that night. I was Sure they would Jump at a chance of that Kind So I went back up on the mountain to Set the traps. I found a bed where a bear had laid in it 13 times [?] that Spring for Six or Seven days. I Searched around for Some distance and found a track I took to be my crippled bear [*wounded June 16*]. I camped out that night.

Thursday June 20 [*22*]

I got out at light and hunted around until 10 oclock for a good Set for another trap. I found Signs in Several places but was Same bear I was working out and no better than the Sets I Knew. I put out one trap at the bed the bear used 13 times and Set the other one on an uncertain Set. One of the triggers got Sprung in Shipping. I fixed it the Very best I could and went on down to camp. Carried a trap to make a Set I found about two miles from camp. I was late getting in that night.

Friday June 21st [*23rd*]

I intended putting the trap out that morning. Doctor Myers asked me to go down the river and See if I could Start a bear. The packer Said he Saw a bear Several days before in the road. We went and Stayed out most all day. We Saw five different tracks that day none of them good enough to Suit Joe and Doc. We found two elk tracks late in the evening about two miles from camp. My dogs took a cold track and then went South out of hearing and back close to camp late in the evening.

Ben Lilly's Tales

Saturday June 22nd [*24th*]
The bear that I brought the trap down to Set for passed through about a three year old. I went out before breakfast and Set the trap and was a day too late. So that was one time my obedience Knocked me out of a bear and it would take 15 days before he would be back again. I took a horse and two bear traps and went up near Elk Mountains and Set the two traps after dark for the big bear. I had found his Stepping path. He was the Same Size of the Taos bear [*the grizzly Ben had tracked the previous summer in northern New Mexico*] and I was Very anxious to get him. His track was Very dim and it was hard to Say if it was a grizzly but chances it was. I was going to lay over up there Sunday and make a hunt for him Monday over the ranges. The horse broke loose and made for camp with a drag rope. I put out after it and tracked it to camp. Flies would Kill a horse in a day if it was tangled and no Smoke.

Sunday June 23rd [*25th*]
Stayed all day in camp when I reached camp.

Monday June 23rd [*26th*]
Went up on Lookout Mountain to the two bear traps I Set on June 20th [*22nd*]. When about two miles away from camp my dogs Struck a fresh bear track made that night. I tied Crook up and went back after Joe Doc and the dogs. Joe was then at camp. He Said the horses was out and Doc was out looking [*for*] fish bait and they would rather not try it. The horses was all up when I left So I went on up to the trap and found a Sheep in the trap and a bear had walked right in the place where the trap was Set. I looked [*up*] the herder and left a check for $5.00. There was quite a herd moved in So I moved the traps out. I dressed the Sheeps wound the best I could. I feel hopeful it will live. There were Several thousand Sheep brought in in different bunches. In fact only little of that Section was not Stocked with large bunches of Sheep.

I went up to my traps near Elk Mountain range where the traps was Set for the big bear. I got them about 4 oclock p.m. I had one dog Crook. He trailed a two year bear down to the trap and [*the bear*] walked right in it. I had Set it Very hard So a medium Sized bear couldnt throw it. I hunted around until night. I found another

Small yearling bears track and it walked over the other trap couldnt throw it. I also found where the big bear passed through going Southeast. This was [at] dark. I came to my camp which was only a frying pan and Saddle blanket.

Tuesday June 25th [27th]
I was out at daylight and I found tracks of the big bear 6 or 8 days old made before a light rain going east and I also found where he went early in Spring going Southeast. I had found a wallow hole of water that he used about twice a month when he comes through this Section. I put one trap in the wallow and one on a Stepping path. I regarded both Sets good ones but would take eight or ten days for him to come. I came back to camp going west then I turned Southwest and went down a davide to the road that led up Silver Creak. I Saw 2 [3?] bear tracks as I came around that way. Two of them was the ones that walked over the traps and the other one was a medium Sized bear. This bear [the big bear] is the Same Size as the bear you [McFadden] chased at Taos New Mexico [in 1921]. This is the largest bear track I have Seen in Idaho. I could have trapped the Smaller bear but I wanted the larger one and fixed the traps So Small bear could not throw them. I met Dr. Myers on the creak fishing and we all came back to the camp late in the evening.

Friday [Wednesday] June 28
I went up near the ranger Station and brought down two bear traps I had left up there. I brought them down So as to be ready to pack up when we made the move. I then hunted up Silver Creak where I had last Seen the Signs of the crippled bear the one I had Shot. I found no fresh Signs and came back to camp that night.

[Thursday, June 29]
We were informed that the Sheep would be in next day and the horses would be Short on grass and we would have to move to Pin [Pen] Basin [located about eight miles east of Warm Lake]. I was Very anxious to Stay and Keep the traps working for the bear or I was willing to help them move and come back and get the traps later. Joe had a Sick dog that he wanted packed on a horse and needed help So I led the horse. I hated to leave the bear as I felt

quite Sure I could do Some good work in another week there. Good hunting in all directions. So I went up after the traps. Crook Struck another trail of a bear.

Saturday June 29th [*Friday, June 30th*]
The camp was all packed for Pen Bason [*Basin*]. We travelled all day and camped on Bull Dog Canion. Saw Some bear Signs on the road while travelling. Struck Snow at night Some old Snow that had not melted.

Sunday June 30th [*Saturday, July 1st*]
We found Snow and bad travelling all before noon. We landed at Pen Bason at Sundown. About 12 or 15 miles is all we can travel in one day. Bad roads and taken almost a half day to get things packed. Then the grass was good.

[*Sunday, July 2nd*]
Next morning it proved to be Monday instead of Sunday and July 2nd So I Stayed in camp for Sunday. First and Second was used in June in moving and dated June 29 and 30.

July 3rd 1922
Was Kept for Sunday. It was Monday.

July 4 1922
Hunted out of Pen Bason. Struck running bear trail a one oclock going east. Dogs got a way from me. I hunted for them until night and failed to hear them at all. I found a yearling bear track that was travelling with the other bear. The first track Struck was apparently a She bear. The yearling had Visited a dead Sheep. I lay out that night.

July 5 1922 Wednesday
I heard Crook and Monk trailing at half past five oclock. I failed to catch up with them and at half past eight oclock Monk came on the yearling bears track the one I had Seen in the evening. I hunted all day for the other three dogs. Found Crook and Rambler at camp. Frank came in that night. I found no more bear tracks that day.

Idaho Hunting Diary

July 6 1922 Thursday
Worked on my Shoes. Worked Some on my diary and made the boys a fish gig and helped them Kill a 14 lb. Salmon and they were to take Some grub up in the mountains for me to Save me time on next day.

July 7 1922 Friday
I hunted up Whiskey Creak [*a small tributary of Johnson Creek*] near the davide. I found a dead grizzly bear that was near two horses. He had been dead for Several months. I think must have been poisoned. I hung his Skull up to Send to you. It was an old male. 5 inch front foot wide and hind foot 9 inches long. He was the Same Size as the one at Taos N.M. I Struck trail of a black She bear and one cub. Trailed them until dark. Lay out all night. Saw a yearling bears tracks.

Saturday July 8 1922
Took up Same trail of the She bear and cub. It was about 4 days old and had trailed continuously west on South Slope of the Mountains the day before and I was only able to See the Cubs track in one place in a half days trailing and today I trailed it full five miles and I found where She the Mother laid up for one day and there the cubs track was Very plain in two places and later on I found it plain in Some ashes and dirt from a burnt tree. I trailed it until late in the evening. They were then going north. I returned to camp expecting to go back Sure Monday morning. I was about 18 miles north of camp at Pen Bason.

July 9 1922 Sunday
Lay over all day in camp. A Sheep man that was lost come by our camp and told us that a bear Killed a Sheep for him about five miles a way.

July 10 1922 Monday
I went east up Whiskey Creak. Struck bear track at head of Whiskey Creak going South east. The man that was trying to tell me where his camp was was lost and I had to hunt up his camp. I found the Sheep late in the evening. The dogs took the bears track and it had

99

Killed a Sheep. It come a rain and rained the track out. I camped right there. It came another rain that night.

July 11 1922 Tuesday
I was up at 3 oclock. Took a round at daylight for the bear. It never come back that night. About one oclock I found the track made during the rain. Dogs trailed it for a while. I Stopped then and came to camp thinking I would get Joe and Some of the dogs and try to Kill it and have Some of the dogs in the race. I got in to camp that night and one of the Game Wardens was in and wanted me to go over on Pistol Creak with him.

July 12 1922 Wednesday
I rode one horse and led a pack horse. We went over to Pistol Creak Ranger Station and Struck camp. I found no bear Signs while I was going over as I was only riding the road.

July 13 1922 Thursday
I took it afoot and hunted east of Big Pistol Creak clear to top of davide laying east of Station and north towards Sammon [*Salmon*] River. I Struck bear tracks in five places. I Saw hair rubbed on trees that came from a light cinnamon and a dark brown bear and had been made five days. They had traveled eastward.

July 14 1922 Friday
The warden and I Started Soon and rode all day west up Little Pistol Creak on east Side in Search of bear and lion Signs. I found 1 bear track about two weeks old going South. I camped out by myself and he went home that night.

July 15 1922 Saturday
I went by Pistol Lake and hunted around all points from camp. Found no tracks of mountain lion or bear. I then drifted South down the trails to our camp at Pen Bason. I had two horses out one with a light pack and one to ride and as we were to move Monday I promised Joe I would get back Saturday evening with the horses. The packer Mr. Sam Cup was in—came in Friday evening. Mr. Sy Johnson the cook went out to Knox to get Some tobacco and other

little things. It was then about 4 oclock P.M.

[*July 16, 1922, Sunday*]
[*Johnson, the cook*] Came back Sunday evening. Sam Cup the packer Spent Sunday trying to pack up Some of the Stuff for moving the following week.

I Saw a man [*earlier in the week*] who was mining near the mouth of Sulphur Creak and I was telling him of finding the grizzly bear that was dead and he was evidently poisoned and he told me a trapper had put out poison and he was Killed in that way. I had found a few hair down on Lightning Creak and brought them out and Showed these to Dr. Myers and Joe. From bites on trees I found I decided a grizzly male bear had made two trips in that Section last Spring and Summer but could find no trace of him this Spring during our last Stay at Peace Valley. I Saw a man that was on Little Pistol Creak and he told me that two years ago he Saw a Very large bear track on little Pistol Creak So I have made a Very close Search in the location he mentioned and found no fresh tracks of a bear of that Size and the man I met when I told him I thought this was the Same bear that I found dead and asked him if they had found a big track this Season and [*he*] Said they had not and every Season he passed regular going each way north and South and he thought I was correct.

I have noticed Very closely for large Sized male bear. There is a big fellow down at Peace Valley east near Elk Mountain. I found when he came out in early Spring and where he made two trips this Spring and where he had wallowed in a regular water hole that he has used for years on his trips through that Section. His track was partly rained out and I was not certain as to whether it was a grizzly . . . [*or*] brown bear but it is the Same Size as the Taos bear in New Mexico . . . and I think a grizzly. [*Here a page of the diary was torn and incomplete.*] This is only guess work from a dim track. I had Set two traps up there for him and one in another . . . intended to work the country out thoroughly to locate . . . . Sheep were brought in and they were . . . to move on . . . horse feed and grazing likely to be . . . at down by the . . . also anxious to Stay with the traps . . . a few days . . . up with the camp but they all objected Saying . . . the move and I could See Very plain . . . I . . . moving.

Ben Lilly's Tales

Monday July 16 [*17*]
Worked on my diary and round camp . . . .

Tuesday July 17th [*18th*]
Moved to Ranger Station on Trout Creak. My dogs Started a trail going through a little Swampy place on Some branches [*small creeks*] I thought was a bear track. I tried to Stop them. They came in after dark to where we were camped for the night.

Wednesday July 18th [*19th*]
Moved down Johnson Creak about Six miles above Yellow Pine. Joe and Slim Said they Saw a bear track in the road. Joe brought me a measure. It was a full grown brown or black Size. I didnt See it. I was driving two loose horses and was traveling ahead of them.

Thursday July 19 [*20*]
It was raining next morning. It cleared off and the packs were all loaded and Struck but we got about a mile from camp and my dogs Struck a bear trail behind us and we failed to Stop them and one of your Airedales went with them. His name was Charley. The dogs got away from me on the river where the water was roaring So I could not hear them. I rode until dark and found no trace of them.

July 20 [*21*] Friday
I Stayed all night and found Frank next morning Crook and Rambler late in the evening. They came in to my old camp where we Stayed the night before. I went to the packers camp. They left me Some dinner and dog feed. I Saw a bear track the boys rode over 4 x 7 1/2 [*inches*]. The packers camp Joe and Slim and all of your dogs were gone. I went back to where I had lost the dogs and found Rambler and Crooks track was there and Monk had been there. I found Crook.

Saturday July 21st [*22nd*]
Hunted all day for Monk. Failed to find him.

Sunday July 22nd [*23rd*]
Lay over at Johnson Creak Bridge where I Saw Monks tracks last all

day and night.

Monday July 23rd [24th]
Monk came in Monday morning. I Started to catch up with the camp. I Struck out to catch camp on Big Creak about one mile north of Yellow Pine. [*Big Creek is about ten miles northeast of Yellow Pine.*] Dogs Struck cold bear trail. They Struck three more tracks that evening in traveling a pack trail. I always Stopped them as Soon as I could. All four of my dogs got away from me that evening. I Stopped Crook. Monk Rambler and Frank was out after a bear. I lay out all night.

Tuesday July 24th [25th]
Rambler came in at 8 oclock A.M. At nine A.M. Monk and Frank came in. I then Started for Big Creak Camp. The dogs Struck a trail in a half a mile of camp and all but Rambler [*ran off*]. I Stopped him. I found them about 10 miles north and got them all together at 12 oclock. I reached the camp at Big Creak late in the evening and found a nice camp erected there and as usual every thing in good Shape.

Wednesday July 25th [26th]
It commenced raining early in the morning. Just enough fell to wet the bushes. On Friday the 20th [*21st*] I was Very Sick with grip [*grippe—influenza*] and had taken a dose of Epsom Salts and it made me Very Sick. I was [*am*] Staying in camp trying to get better and posting my diary up.

Joe and Slim take the dogs out every day at about two oclock and travel them in the roads or trails until about 5 oclock. After Joe came back he took his rifle and went down to Set for a coyote he Saw while exercising the dogs and was watching for the coyote [*when*] he Saw a bear. He Shot at it five times. I told him I would help him find his bear next day. I was getting worse all of the time. I decided to take two pills next thing at bed time So I took them and lay down.

Thursday July 26th [27th]
I tried to get up next morning before day and I was So weak I could

not Stand up. The pills made me Very Sick and the grip too with the medicine laid me out. I Just couldnt Stay up and had to give the hunt up. Joe and Slim took Lilly Cricket Cliff and two trig dogs and Several others and went up where he Shot [at] the bear. Found no blood. Lilly took a track and ran off. Cricket got full of porcupine quills. They came back in three hours disgusted with bear hunting. Lilly came in hearing of camp and was only heard two or three barks So She Lilly came in at eleven oclock. Joe and Slim took the grand exercising parade with the dogs as usual. The dogs are in fine Shape but getting no hunting at all.

Friday July 27th [*28th*]
I was Still Sick. Trying to write a little on my diary and piddle a little around camp. At 12 oclock I took Monk and Frank out to look for bear and lion tracks. I went South of a prong of Big Creak that came in at the camp. I Saw one coyote. Shot and wounded it. I went up on mountain Side and head reaches of canions then back on West davides north. Found a female bears tracks Just before dark about one mile away from camp. I trailed on it until dark. Took dogs off and came in to camp.

Saturday July 28th [*29th*]
I took Crook Frank and Monk and went north up on a mountain Side where Joe thought he had found a large Very old bears track that had been made a long time Since Spring. He thought it might be made by a bear. I failed to find any thing I thought was made by a big bear. I Saw a four inch wide bear track that had been made about 8 days old. I Stayed out until dark looking for lion tracks and bear tracks. I passed a big lake and lots of high bluffs that was Suitable for mountain lions but no Signs. A young man Said he Saw a lion east of these rocks I was on and described it as being a gray color and Said he had a 38 gun but didnt Shoot at it. Said it crawled upon a rock and laid down and looked at him. I am afraid he Saw a coyote instead of a lion. He Saw that two weeks ago. Joe and Slim takes the dogs over the trail he Saw the cougar on every day on their exercising parade.

Idaho Hunting Diary

Sunday July 29th [*30th*]
Lay over in camp all day. Joe and Slim Saw a black bear while out exercising the dogs. Came back and got two more men. Tied up a few of the dogs and Saw this bear when they got back. They turned dogs loose on it in a few minutes. They ran pretty then all got Scattered and Some ran after a gray wolf Joe Said and Some came back to camp. I was in hopes they would get it but failed. It was a Small black bear.

[Bear sign observed from May to July 1922]

Pen Bason on Johnson Creak Idaho, Johnson Ranger Station

1 female bear barren She bear	1
1 female yearling bear	1
2 female and cub	2
1 yearling female bear	1
1 male two year old	1

On Pistol Creak Ranger Station locality

1 yearling male bear on Little Pistol Creak	1
2 one brown bear 1 cinnamon light color female and yearling	2
[*Total*]	9

Tracks that I Saw and examined closely from the 27th day of May until the 30th day of July 1922 hunting for Mr. W. H. McFadden Ponca City Oklahoma from Banks Idaho to Big Creak Idaho the head reaches of Big Creak. I am quite Sure I have counted 39 tracks that were all different bear.

Bear tracks found in coming from Pen Bason to Big Creak Idaho

1 female dogs trailed on Johnson Creak	1
1 2 year old male bear on east fork [*of the South Fork* *of the*] Sammond [*Salmon River*] north of Yellow Pine	1
1 bear track grown Size on east fork Sammon. Not plain	1

Ben Lilly's Tales

enough to tell Sex.
2 yearling bear tracks on Profile Canion one male and 2
one female
1 female bear tracks Very old and Small looks 2 year old 1
1 yearling bear Small female 1
1 2 year old female bear at Big Creak.. 1
1 2 year old male track at Big Creak.. <u>1</u>
[*Total*] 9

Peace Valley Silver Creak Idaho

1 male bear 2 year old... 1
2 female bear and yearling.. 2
1 three year old male bear... 1
1 two year old female bear.. 1
1 four year old brown male bear... 1
3 two yearlings 1 female bear 3

Elk Mountain davide east & South of Peace Valley

1 large male track 5 inches wide 9 inches long 1
1 Small female yearling bear 1
1 two year old male bear.. <u>1</u>
[*Total*] 12

1 Bear track found near Banks 2 year old male 1

Near Garden Valley Lightning Creak Camp Idaho

1 2 year old male bear... 1
1 grown female bear.. 1
2 yearlings 1 female 1 male bear 2
1 2 year old male bear... 1
1 2 year old female.. 1
1 barren She female 1
1 four year old male. This bear made only one trip
in while I was there... <u>1</u>
[*Total*] 9

Idaho Hunting Diary

[*The diary continues.*]

Monday July 30th according to my diary count. 31st camp count.
I am trying to get my diary ready to mail today. One of the cooks is going out tomorrow. We are expecting to move my camp and Some Stuff down the creak and in a day or So the rest will follow with the balance of the camp.

Tuesday 8 1 1922
Packed up and moved 12 miles down Big Creak.

Wednesday 8 2 1922
Packed up and moved about 12 miles down Big Creak.

Thursday 8 3 1922
Hunted up Rainey [*Ramey*] Creak. Trailed two year old bears going east. Quit them late in the evening at the head of Rainey Creak.

Friday 8 4 1922
Rained in the morning. I went out at 12 oclock and Struck trail of two bear going east. Quit it late in the evening on Crooked Creak.

Saturday 8 5 1922
Hunted down Big Creak and up Crooked Creak. Found one track.

Sunday
Stayed all day in camp. It rained Several Showers that day.

Monday 7th
All pack up to move camp until two oclock. I Stayed to take care of things in camp. When a part of camp is moved the packer is to be back after the camp day after tomorrow.

Tuesday 8 8 1922
Hunted on South Side and east of Big Creak from camp. Found Sign of two bear a male and a female and a cub. The tracks was too old to work.

Ben Lilly's Tales

Wednesday 9th
Waited for packer to come in to move camp until 12 oclock then took around up the creak on east Side. Found no tracks.

Thursday 10th
Stayed in a part of the day waiting for the packer. Hunted up creak on north Side. Packer came in late.

Friday 11th 1922
Packed up and moved up to Cottonwood Basin. Left Camp at half past nine in the morning. Got there at 4 oclock in evening. I put up my tent at late evening. Saw 1 bear track.

Saturday the 12th
Hunted back where I Saw the track. It was a two year old. Crook and Monk took the trail trailed it about a mile and got it much fresher. They Soon got out of hearing. I was using Frank as a guide and he couldnt find the dogs. I hunted until 8 oclock. Come two rains during the day. In evening it is Sundown and they are Still out.

Sunday the 13th of August 1922
Lay over in Camp. Crook came in at 4 oclock P M.

Monday August 14 1922
Monk came in at 8 A M. Joe and I took Rambler and rode down east on one branch of cottonwood [Creek]. Struck another branch of Cottonwood and turned upstream going Southeast. Found elk tracks and deer tracks. It rained. We hunted down Stream. Saw Small bear tracks going down north. We went down to tool box on Cottonwood meadow and then back to camp that evening.

Tuesday August 15
I took pack on my back three dogs Crook Monk and Rambler and Struck out east in Search of bear and lion tracks. I hunted principally on davides and canions. Saw elk tracks in three places. One male that was rubbing his horns on bushes and Smaller Size track along the marsh. Stayed all night on east Side of davide next to Samon River on head reaches of a canion that run into Samon River.

Idaho Hunting Diary

Wednesday 8 16 1922
Hunted north up davide east and then north. Took down high davide leading northwest. Found a track of a bear going Southeast. Found two tracks. One 2 year old female and one female that I thought has cubs following. The dogs trailed on little poles [?] was why I thought She had a cub following.

Thursday 8 17 1922
Struck track close to camp going South. I thought was one I was trailing in the evening. I took dogs off and hunted up northeast. Found fresh old tracks large one. I then turned down west and found trail of female and cub going Southwest. Trailed her until Corning and dogs charged off on a barren She bear track. It was getting late and I had to Stop them. I camped.

Friday 8 18
I hunted west. Dogs Struck female yearling bear track going west and it was too cold to trail. I Saw where it made two trips in one pond. I took dogs out and tried to find She and cub. I wanted to catch the cub alive but come a big rain and dogs Struck trail of another bear a barren She and we had rain and had to Stop for night.

Saturday 8 19
I was out of provisions. No food for myself or dogs. I tried to take hunt for the She and cub. I Kept the dogs tied to me. I Struck track of the barren She bear fresh. It Soon come a rain and it rained it out So I had to make my way west to Camp. Dogs Struck track of Small bear late in evening where Joe and I Saw it Monday. It was rained out So they could not Keep it going. It was late in evening. I got to camp. I was out 5 days. Saw 3 elk tracks 6 deer. 2 does 3 fawns 1 3 point buck. 8 bear tracks.

Sunday 8 20 22
Lay over all day in camp at Cottonwood. Fair and clear.

Monday 8 21
Joe and I went north then west on big davide running north from camp at popus [*Papoose*] meadows on Cottonwood [*Creek*]. We

Ben Lilly's Tales

turned South going east Side of Doubtful [*Disappointment?*] canion. Came a rain at 12 oclock and every thing was Very wet. We hunted back east and South to camp. It rained more.

Tuesday 8 22 1922
I took the No. 5 bear traps on my back and Some provisions and Set them about 12 miles east of this camp where I found the yearling bear track and the barren She and She and cub. I found no fresh Signs of bear except the yearling. The other three bear Seemed to be gone. I found fresh tracks of the little one. I Set the two traps out that night after dark. Went about a quarter of a mile and camped that night.

[*At this point there is a gap in Ben Lilly's diary.*]

October 13 1922 Friday
I think we moved back to your main camp a Cottonwood. I went up to where we had two bear and I brought them into camp.

October 14
I think Dr. Myers Joe Slim [*Vernon*] Caldwell and myself went bear hunting and Mr. McFadden and Jack Smith went elk hunting on Cave Creak. We Struck bear trail about two miles east of camp. Very cold. The others rode on and Soon Struck a fresh track. Vernons two dogs Soon treed it and he Killed it. I never turned my dogs loose. Struck 4 or 8 tracks that day. I was trying to find the dogs that ran off.

October 15 1922
Sunday. Lay over in camp. I helped Skin the bear.

October 16 1922
Monday. We Struck out the Same route for bear and never Struck a trail until ten oclock. I Struck 3 tracks a female a yearling and a two year old and only had three dogs and each dog took a track of his own. They were Soon out of hearing. Crook came by and he Soon Jumped his and was north down Hungry Creak and Joe and Caldwell had both packs of dogs with them. They hadnt got a Start. Crook ran

close up to them and they got all of the dogs in. They come in Sight of me and they then turned north and northwest. They run the bear until a way in the night. There was two dogs running at nine oclock that night. I heard Frank Still running as I come in that night and could hear two more dogs running but I could not locate them. Joe came in that evening and heard Frank running as he come in.

October 17 1922
Tuesday. I took Some provisions and Started back to See if I could find Vernon Caldwell Dr. Myers and Slim or any of the dogs. I was off at light but every thing was quiet. Mr. McFadden and Smith had heard the dogs after dark So we all was in the chase. They Stopped Some of the dogs and Some could not be Stopped. We gathered all of the dogs that was out that day but two one of Caldwells and one of mine. Found Dr. Myers and Vernon Caldwell. Stayed back to find the two dogs which they got them both. Some hunters had tied them and was taking them away. The Doctor and Vernon overtook us at Henderson where we waited for them.

October 18 Wednesday
Moved from McFadden camp head reaches of Cottonwood [*Creek*] to Crookard [*Crooked*] Creak.

October 19 1922 Thursday
Drove from Crookard Creak to Big Creak. Camped at Old Cabin.

October 20 Friday
Drove from camp on Big Creak to Edwardsburg. Camped at Edwardsburg.

October 21 Saturday
Drove from Edwardsburg to Paradise. Camped at Paradise.

October 22 Sunday 1922
Sunday Started from Camp at Paradise and come by Yellow Pine and Stopped over at Henderson.

Ben Lilly's Tales

October 23 Monday
I helped Mr. McFadden. He mended his gun Stock.

October 24 Tuesday
I went up on the mountains looking for bear Signs. Found where one had been caught and got away and where another big one run from the men. It had been done two weeks. I also found 2 other fresher bear tracks one two year old and a full grown She. I come in at nine or ten oclock that night. It was Very dark and drizzling rain.

That Same night Mr. McFaddens favorite hound Lilly was Sick and only lived a few minutes when we commenced to doctor her. On examination we found an abscess in the Stomach and a hole in it about the Size of a lead pencil. The bloody water had passed through and Showed both inside the Stomach and connecting bowels and bloody water had worked its way through the holes in the Stomach and filled the inside of the body with bloody water. We buried her on Henderson place in a little grave dug with a Spade and two rocks Set up at each end. She was a true type of a bright red fox hound Very trim. Made a fine trailer with a beautiful Voice and used it continuously either trailing or running and had numbers of Scars on her that was made by bear. She was a dog that any hunter would be proud of in appearance. She was perfect as a hound and could rank with mixed blood dogs for Speed or with terriers or airedales for Speed or grit and would run all day alone or in a pack. She could not have been bought at any price.

Ranger was a Very desirable bear dog. He was 12 years old and Still a good worker. He was Killed by a porcupine on Lightning Creak. We hunted him for Several days and couldnt find. He was afterwards found by cow men. He was blind. The porcupine quills were Stuck in his eyes. I found his track close to the porcupine but could not find him. I was at that place three times different days. I guess he had rambled off and was not able to locate himself or travel. The porcupine was a Very large one and they drag it over Several logs a distance of 25 Steps and the quills had Stuck in the logs and in three or four more dogs that made their way to camp and I think our airedale never did Show up. The Middle River [*Middle Fork of the Payette River*] was Very Swift and brush upon banks. It puzzled a dog in good Shape to make it across account of rapid current and brush. There was a reward offered but none had heard of him. We were told after we moved that two men hunting cattle Stopped under a tree in a Shower of rain and one of their dogs Kept running under the hill and barked at Something. They went to See what it was and it was Ranger and he was blinded by porcupine quills. They pulled them out and tried to lead him out. He led a little ways and dropped dead. It was about two weeks Since he was missing. He must have Suffered. My tracks was in 40 yards of where he was found. I hunted and blowed the horn for him. I guess he did not Know how to travel and did not bark. I Saw his track close to the porcupine. He was on the bear track there and I looked everywhere I thought he would be likely to go. I was under the impression that the coyotes had got after him and he had gone out Some of the . . . to Keep from Swimming the river. It is hard to Say whether he wandered around or Just give up and laid down. I Know I wandered in many places in different directions and failed to find his tracks. I could have missed him if he Kept Still. I think the dogs would have found his tracks if he had moved about.

Cricket a Very fine bear dog was lost on a chase when Mr. McFadden and Some of the men was out about the first of October. She was A 1 and well broke for bear. Three of the best [*dogs*] that could be had [*were lost*]. The picks of different bear packs of dogs in different Sections and did extra good work in 1921 on the last years hunt.

6

PHOTOGRAPHS AND DRAWINGS

Louisiana, East Texas, and Chihuahua

Ben Lilly and his second wife, Mary Sisson Lilly, at the time of their marriage in 1891. The couple made their home at Mer Rouge, Louisiana. Ben wore a full beard his entire adult life. Courtesy of Fay Bowe, Mer Rouge.

Photographs and Drawings

Ben was forty-nine years old and living in East Texas when this portrait was taken in December 1906. Photo by John Strickrott. M. H. Salmon Collection.

Ben Lilly's Tales

Ben Lilly waits to ambush a Big Thicket bear. His rifle is a Winchester Model 1894. Photo taken in East Texas in December 1906 by John Strickrott. Reproduced from the September-October 1943 issue of Arizona Highways.

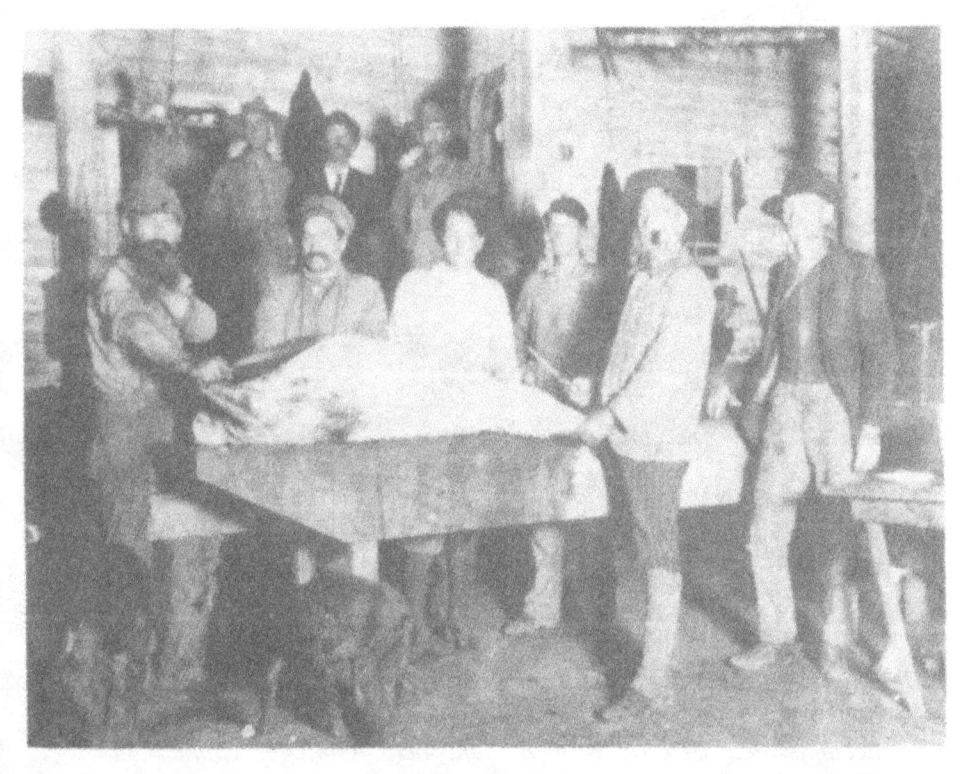

Photographs and Drawings

Hunters butcher a bear killed in the Big Thicket of East Texas. The bearded man at the left is believed to be Ben Lilly. Photo taken in December 1906 by John Strickrott. M. H. Salmon Collection.

Ben Lilly's Tales

Ben Lilly with a grizzly. Information written on the back of a very old print of this photo indicates that it was taken in 1910 by Frank Sanborn, a Mexico City businessman and sport hunter who accompanied Ben on a bear hunt near Gallego, Chihuahua.[53] Gallego is a station on the railroad about eighty miles north of Chihuahua City and is near the southern tip of the grizzly's range in North America. This grizzly's skull (that of an adult male) must be the one Lilly shipped from Gallego to the U.S. National Museum in November 1910. The bear was reportedly killed eleven miles west of Gallego. Lilly didn't send the bear's skin to the museum—it was probably kept by Sanborn for a trophy.[54] Courtesy of Frank C. Hibben and M. H. Salmon.

Photographs and Drawings

West Texas, New Mexico, and Arizona

A studio portrait taken in El Paso about 1911. Reproduced from the September-October 1943 issue of Arizona Highways.

Another studio image of Ben, possibly taken at the same time as the previous photo. Courtesy of Fay Bowe, Mer Rouge, Louisiana.

Photographs and Drawings

The lions and bears were in considerable danger when Ben Lilly took to the trail. Ben's rifle appears to be a Winchester '94. Reproduced from Young and Goldman 1946.

Ben Lilly's Tales

Ben Lilly and lady friends at Mogollon, New Mexico. Reproduced from Hoover 1958.

Photographs and Drawings

Ready for a hunt. Reproduced from the July 1923 issue of American Forestry.

Ben Lilly's Tales

Reproduced from the August 1938 issue of American Forests.

Photographs and Drawings

Courtesy of Warren White, Mer Rouge, Louisiana.

Ben Lilly's Tales

Ben and four of his finest hounds. Left to right: Jack, Crook, Tip, Queen. Photo taken by J. S. Ligon about 1917. M. H. Salmon Collection.

Photographs and Drawings

The master hound man and a "good" mountain lion. Reproduced from the January 1920 issue of Illustrated World *magazine.*

Ben Lilly's Tales

Lilly sometimes rode a burro or mule between hunting camps, but once in the game country he usually hunted on foot. Reproduced from the September-October 1943 issue of Arizona Highways.

Photographs and Drawings

Photo taken by J. S. Ligon about 1917. Silver City Museum No. 542.

Ben Lilly's Tales

Courtesy of Manuel Gutierrez.

Photographs and Drawings

This photo was taken in 1916 or early 1917 at a ranch in the Blue River country of eastern Arizona. Ben (right) is stretching out the skin of a large male lion. The young mountain lion (alive) below the skin was due to be sent to Washington, D.C., presumably to be placed in a zoo (see Appendix A, "Letters to J. Stokley Ligon"). Silver City Museum No. 763.

Ben Lilly's Tales

A greeting card featuring Ben, his hounds, and a pet mountain lion—possibly the same cat as in the previous photo. Silver City Museum No. 750.

Photographs and Drawings

Silver City Museum No. 879.

Ben Lilly's Tales

Ben and his dogs at the G.O.S. Ranch headquarters about twenty miles north of Silver City. Ben's rifle is a Model 99 Savage. Silver City Museum No. 759.

Photographs and Drawings

Norm Woolsey (born in 1922) was a boy living with his parents in Cliff, New Mexico, when he had his only encounter with Ben Lilly. The year was about 1930. Norm and his father, Lars Walter Woolsey, went to the general store one day and found Ben there. The famous hunter had come out of the mountains for supplies, and a crowd had gathered to hear of his latest exploits. Ben gave the elder Woolsey a print of this photo about that time, and Norm has it now. In it Ben poses with his hounds near the headquarters of the G.O.S. Ranch on upper Sapillo Creek. Courtesy of Norman G. Woolsey, Mesa, Arizona.

Ben Lilly's Tales

A group of Biological Survey employees talk things over in the Gila high country. Left to right: J. B. "Jack" Thompson, Ben Lilly, Walter W. Hotchkiss, J. Stokley Ligon. This photo, which dates from about 1920, may have been taken by Ligon using a camera with a timed shutter. M. H. Salmon collection. (The identities of the men in this photo were confirmed in 1998 by Johnny Thompson, Jack Thompson's son.)

Photographs and Drawings

Ben Lilly and Albert Pickens. Courtesy of Manuel Gutierrez.

Emmett Goforth, his father, Andrew Jackson Goforth, and Ben Lilly with mountain lion kittens. Photo taken by Leslie Goforth (Emmett's brother) in 1921 at the Goforth home on Sapillo Creek (near Lake Roberts). Courtesy of Gila Cliff Dwellings National Monument. Original print donated by Beth Turner.

Photographs and Drawings

Ben Lilly with a mountain lion kitten in downtown Silver City. He and his pet are in front of Howell Drugs located on the northeast corner of Bullard and Broadway. Silver City Museum No. 101. Original print donated by Mrs. Robert Jackson in 1965.

Ben Lilly's Tales

Reproduced from Young and Goldman 1946.

Photographs and Drawings

Ben searches the horizon on Christmas Day 1931. Photo taken at the G.O.S. Ranch headquarters in the Gila National Forest. Silver City Museum No. 590. Original print donated by Hal Cooley.

Ben Lilly in old age. Courtesy of Billy Joe Collyge, Silver City.

Photographs and Drawings

Ben Lilly's Drawings

A mountain lion and bear as rendered by Ben. Reproduced from The Ben Lilly Legend *by J. Frank Dobie (1950). Courtesy of Little, Brown and Company, Boston.*

Ben Lilly's Tales

More fanciful Ben Lilly drawings. Courtesy of Sandel Library, Northeast Louisiana University, Monroe.

Photographs and Drawings

Envelopes decorated by Ben. Reproduced from The Ben Lilly Legend *by J. Frank Dobie (1950). Courtesy of Little, Brown and Company, Boston.*

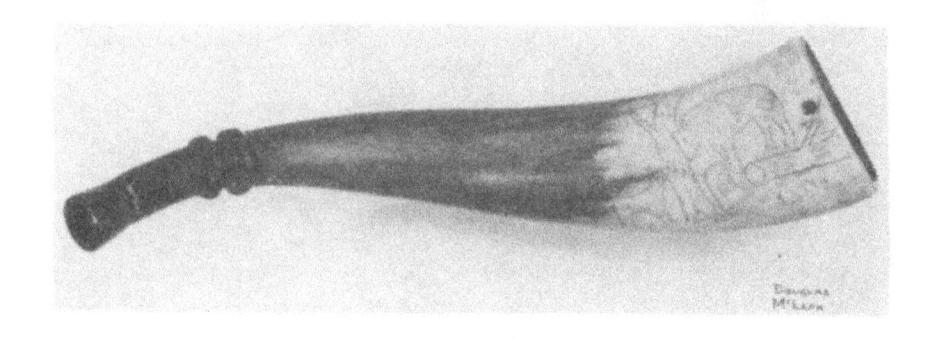

Top: one of Ben's homemade blowing horns. Bottom: detail drawing of the scrimshaw-like carving on the horn. Reproduced from The Ben Lilly Legend *by J. Frank Dobie (1950). Courtesy of Little, Brown and Company, Boston.*

Photographs and Drawings

Another Ben Lilly bear. Courtesy of Manuel Gutierrez.

EDITOR'S AFTERWORD
THE BEN LILLY MEMORIALS

Two monuments of bronze and stone have been erected honoring Ben Lilly: one (1947) in the Gila National Forest north of Silver City, New Mexico, and another (1997) in the town of Mer Rouge, Louisiana. A third has been discussed—this proposed memorial would be placed in the Tensas Bayou country in northeastern Louisiana and would commemorate Lilly's 1907 bear hunt with Teddy Roosevelt. But why is all this attention being paid to a man such as Ben Lilly? Why do people find him worthy of statues and monuments?

At first glance these questions seem hard to answer. Ben Lilly didn't achieve the status during his life that commonly inspires later admiration. He wasn't a military leader or popular politician. He didn't discover a rich mine or build a railroad. Ben killed an impressive number of mountain lions and bears (no one knows exactly how many) and thus helped tame the Southern swamps and Western rangelands, but so did other hunters, most of whom are now forgotten. No, it isn't the war he waged against stock-killing animals that makes Ben Lilly interesting. We must look elsewhere to discover his appeal.

Upon reflection it seems clear that Ben Lilly's most significant achievement was the creation of his own legend. The talkative Lilly laid the ground work, then after his death other storytellers enlarged his persona to Paul Bunyan proportions. Rural people loved to gather at the general store and discuss Ben's escapades, often adding anecdotes from their own imaginations. Urban writers couldn't resist describing and embellishing the adventures of the greatest hunter of them all. For decades readers have been fascinated by the saga of "the last of the mountain men." We seem to need larger-than-life heros, even if, in reality, they did not achieve half of their purported feats.

Ben's eccentricities gave support to the fabulous tales people told about him. He truly wasn't an ordinary fellow. In his later years he really did live in the woods, seeking shelter from storms in caves and under overhanging rocks. No matter how severe the weather, Ben stubbornly refused to sleep indoors. His dogs were his companions and hunting with them was his life. Even Teddy Roosevelt was captivated by this singular hunter who was so at home in the wilderness. And who knows what woodcraft skills such a man might possess? Maybe most of the stories told about him are true after all. Maybe he could tell a bear's complete history from a single paw print. Maybe he could shoot the bill off a flying duck with his rifle. Maybe he did slay vicious bears with his hunting knife. A woodsman of Lilly's experience and determination might be able to do many things other hunters could not. His unusual, enigmatic life was the perfect foundation upon which to build a heroic folklore. People have gotten untold pleasure from the Ben Lilly legend. No wonder they have erected more monuments to honor Ben than they have to perpetuate the memory of most governors, senators, or university presidents.

◇ ◇ ◇ ◇ ◇

Eleven years after Ben Lilly's death, this plaque honoring him was placed on a boulder in the Gila National Forest a few miles north of Silver City, New Mexico. The inscription reads: "1856—BEN V. LILLY—1936. Born in Alabama and reared in Mississippi, BEN V. LILLY in early life was a farmer and trader in Louisiana, but turned to hunting of panthers and bears with a passion that led him out of swamps and canebrakes, across Texas, to tramp the wildest mountains of Mexico, and finally become a legendary figure and dean of wilderness hunters in the Southwest. He was a philosopher, keen observer, naturalist, a cherisher of good hounds, a relier on his rifle, and a handicraftsman in horn and steel. He loved little children and vast solitudes. He was a pious man of singular honesty and fidelity and a strict observer of the Sabbath. New Mexico mountains were his final hunting range and the charms of the Gila Wilderness held him to the end. Erected 1947 by friends." Among those involved in the memorial project were writer J. Frank Dobie, former Gila National Forest supervisor Fred Winn, Lilly's old Biological Survey boss J. Stokley Ligon, and Tom Harp of Mer Rouge, Louisiana. Others who helped bring the project to fruition were New Mexico residents Melvin Porterfield, Harry Hickel, and Lloyd Wall.[55] Photo courtesy of David E. Brown, Phoenix.

Afterword

Ken Wyatt puts the finishing touches on a monument to Ben Lilly erected in front of the Mer Rouge, Louisiana, post office in May 1997. The bronze figures include Ben Lilly with two hounds (center), a mountain lion (left) and a bear (right). The inscription reads: "'BEN AND THE BOYS.' 1856 Ben V. Lilly 1936. Like Esau, Jacob's brother of Bible times, Ben Lilly was the ultimate hunter ... but never on Sunday. Not one to focus on acquiring "things" and money, Ben acquired knowledge, knowledge about the outdoors and the four-legged challenges he found there ... mainly bears and lions. Cotton and cattle were soon phased out of his life. Starting a few miles east of here on Bayou Bonne Idee and Beouf River, he, with his dogs, hunted South through Tensas swamp, where President Teddy Roosevelt came to hunt with him, then on West through East Texas, Northern Mexico and ultimately to Southwest New Mexico, where he settled down to do his "patriotic duty" ... kill the mountain lions and bears that killed the ranchers' livestock. The ranchers paid him, the government paid him, unlike back home in Louisiana, so he stayed. He sent the money back home to his wife and children, who lived two blocks North of this monument. One of his two daughters, Verna, became a school teacher of note. At her death in 1985 she bequeathed over a half-million dollars, in two

trust funds, to the Mer Rouge Methodist Church. One fund supports two student scholarships each year, the other, the pastor's salary. Ben Lilly, after a bout with pneumonia, died and was buried in Silver City, N.M. at the age of 80, never having been back to Mer Rouge, but leaving his mark here and across the Southwest." The monument was first proposed in 1992 by the late Jim Rider, a writer for The Bastrop Daily Enterprise *newspaper. It was financed through the efforts of the Mer Rouge Lions Club. A committee led by Warren White raised $11,000 to pay for the sculpture, the plaque, and the masonry base.[56] Photo courtesy of Warren White.*

A close-up view of the bronze sculpture atop the Ben Lilly memorial in Mer Rouge, Louisiana. Courtesy of The Bastrop (La.) Daily Enterprise.

Appendix A

LETTERS FROM BEN LILLY TO FRIENDS AND COLLEAGUES

Letter to A. K. Fisher

Editor's note: Dr. Albert K. Fisher was a senior member of the Biological Survey's Washington staff. Other people mentioned in Ben Lilly's letter are: Dr. C. Hart Merriam, the most influential mammal taxonomist in America and chief of the Biological Survey from its inception in 1885 until he retired in 1910; J. Stokley Ligon, Albuquerque-based supervisor of the Biological Survey's predator control programs in Arizona and New Mexico; Ned Hollister, a Biological Survey naturalist who met Lilly in Louisiana in 1904 and recruited the houndsman to collect specimens of mammals and birds for the U.S. National Museum. The following letter, written while Lilly was camped in the wilderness just west of the Arizona/New Mexico line, was received at the Washington office of the Biological Survey on April 28, 1916. It was first published in *Hunting American Bears* by Frank C. Hibben, 1996 edition.

◇ ◇ ◇ ◇ ◇

Clifton Arizona 4 21 1916
Dr. A. K. Fisher

Dear Friend

I am to day Sending Dr. C. Hart Meriam [*Merriam*] a full grown mountain lion [*specimen*] a male. He was Killed about 20 miles north west of Clifton on a large cluster of Bluffs and deep canion that ran down to Eagle Creak. The Spur Cross ranch is on the canion

Ben Lilly's Tales

west of where I Killed him. I Killed him on wednesday evening before the first of April after a 2 days chase on trail and I found that He had 2 warts on him one under the center of the chin and one in front of the ear. I have never Seen a wart on any of the cat tribe So I thought it would be a good thing to Send the hide and Skull in for Studye at the Museum. Let me Know if it has ever occured on a lion before. He was Very fat and healthy looking.

I come down to Clifton to meet Mr. Ligon and he wired me that He would meet me at NO— Ranch near Double Circle Ranch on Eagle Creak Arizona about 25 miles west of Clifton Arizona. I Killed the 5 lions that I Spoke of Seeing their tracks. This is 99 lions and 30 bear. I Saw 2 bear tracks while I was trailing my last lion and a Very large male lions track on the red hill below Caspers [*Toles Cosper's Y Bar Y*] Ranch [*in Arizona's Blue River country*]. I have been trying to get in that Section for 2 years. I guess I will break up that den. Now it is dark and I have no light. So good night.

Mr. Ligon will come through horse back and expects to meet me on the 2d of April [*May?*]. [*Ligon met with Ben Lilly and hired him to hunt mountain lions for the Biological Survey.*] The 5 lions I Killed had Killed Several head of cattle. There was a Jaguar Killed about 2 years ago on the red hills about 5 miles South of Caspers [*Cosper's*]. It was a male. The hide made in a rug measures 96 inches from tip of tail to End of nose and was 32 inches across the bodeye from one Side to the other. Several men claims that there is another large track been Seen of a leopard as they call it or a over grown Size lion in the Same Section but you know there is but a few men that doesnt find Something out of the main line of animals. I will be in that Section in a few days and will make a Special look out for Sighn. I Saw where the lions had Killed a yearling and there was Some dung covered up there that was rather large. But I Saw Some in Mexico that Size and that track in Mexico front foot measured 3 and 5/8 of an inch across the ball of front foot. My dog got poisoned on that trip and I didnt Kill the animal. That could have been a Jaguar. It was near the head of Caramoa [*El Corazero?*] River in the Taranatras [*Tinaja Lisa?*] Mts between gyago [*Gallego*] and a ranch called Santa Clarra [*Clara*] North of Chiwawa [*Chihuahua*] City. So I will look close around the Red Mts [*thirty miles north of Clifton*] for tracks. I Killed the lion I was trailing

Appendix A

when I found this yearling Killed and it was night and I was out of provisions and 2 dogs lost that was after another one and then was poison out and I hunted the dogs up and then I came out to meet Mr. Ligon. There was a leopard Seen 3 years ago on the west side of the Mogaloon [*Mogollon*] Mts [*in New Mexico*] on the head of dry prong [*Big Dry Creek*] and He [*a rancher?*] has been missing things [*livestock?*]. Are Some chances that this is the Same one [*jaguar*] that was Killed in the red mountain [*a few miles to the west in Arizona*]. If I continue to work that Section I will find out if there is more in there.

I am writing you for fear Dr. C. Hart Marriam might be a way and the wart on the lion skin might be over looked or cut off not Knowing the intention of my Sending the hide. I will write you more fully soon. I am at that calf and have about 20 miles to go a foot through the mts and it is threatening rain. I will make it in about 6 hours. I have done most of this writing almost in the dark after night fall and before day. Kindest regards to Dr. C. Hart Merriam and all of the others. Regards to Mr. Ned Holister [*Hollister*]. I wish you could take a hunt with me. I have Some Very good lion hounds now. I am crazy to get after that old big bear. But I am getting Seventy five dollars and better for mountain lions and it looks like I cant Stop. I would mutch rather hunt big bear but there is more money in lions at the price I am getting.

I thank you Very mutch for Sending Mr. Ligon around to See me. I will do all I can to assist your enterprise. Your best friend

B. V. Lilly

**Two Letters to J. Stokley Ligon,
Ben Lilly's Biological Survey Boss in Albuquerque**

Blue Arizona March 9.1917
Mr J S Ligon Dear Friend

I received yours of the 14 feb a day or So ago and as I have Just been cleaning up a big 7 ft 2 inch male mt Lion hide I will write you this evening. I am Sure I was glad to hear from you. I felt like you had la grip [*grippe or flu*] as it is So Common at that Season. I am real glad you are up.

I was So anxious to meet Dr Fisher. I cant help but feel real anxious to have a hunt with Him and feel like my hunting will not be finished Satisfactory to me if we did not get to get a hunt togather as we have planed one for a long time and you Know my fault is to hang on to the last. So I feel hopeful that we will get to meet each other [and] get in the wild woods. Keep a look out for Jaguars as the Dr is anxious to get one. [*In 1918 Dr. A. K. Fisher came out to New Mexico from Washington and hunted with Ben in the Black Range.*]

I hope you will get to make a hunting trip with me when it is convient for you and get the Kind of Pictures that you are interested in. Write me Just what you are most anxious to have and I can Keep you Posted as to when and where there might be hopes of Such Success. I have 5 or 6 different hunts on foot now and it is hard to Say Just what one I will be at when I hear from you. Every one Seems to be anxious to have me work their Sections. I have been a little Slow a bout taking up work as it was properable you would nead me and the people here would think that I was treating them wrong if I moved a way to work and not finish their work. I told them that you would be apt to put Some one on their ranges if they neaded it to work it over. The Snows ran Several lions down on the ranges. They have been Killing Stock and deer. The last 2 I trailed one Killed 2 deer and the other Killed 3.

It may be that Some of my mail does not reach me as it is Kindness of the Neighbors to try to get it to me and Some times they fail to reach me and it has been So. I am moving So mutch that they cant Keep up with me So a Safe way is to Say Reserve [*New Mexico*] or Blue [*Arizona*]. I guess I will be near blue for 2 weeks or a week at least. You mentioned a bout the Navajoe Blanket. Let me Suggest that you wait until mid Summer and then you may catch a chance to pick up one at a bargain 2nd hand or aneye Kind. I am in no hury and dont you hury about it. Rest easy and pick chances for a bargain.

I have a picture of the little lion and the dogs and the hide of the 7 ft [*one*] that you got last with the head not Skined out. The head in the fork of a tree. Me holding it Stretched out in a tree the little lion and dogs a round. I have 4 or 5 diferent ones that as Soon as I can have Some taken I can give you Some. I am getting pretty good

Bounty now in the Blue Section but will get your other hide that is due as Soon as con venient. I have orders for 4 or 5 big male lions now and I have 4 Big ones on hand. The one Just cleaned up To day is a beauty ful one. He was fat Smooth and Slick. The last hide I Shipped you was frozed for a month and I couldnt Salt it. It got in that Shape while I was carrying the little lion to alpine. So you can See I was not careless. It was unavoidable. I guess it reached you Safe and Sound.

Anaye time you can conveniently reach me come around and Join me and have a real out of doors outing. The first chance I get I will write Dr Fisher and we will try to locate a few Jaguars Some where. Ask King to find out if He can [*find*] Some place where they are reported and I will try to look up the matter and locate them. They are Some in North west Mexico but it is imprudent to work that Section now.

Hoping to See you Soon and have a good time

Yours Truly

B. V. Lilly

[*P.S.*] As I came back from Alpine when I went up I Saw 4 lofer woolf tracks on the head of Camel [*Campbell*] Blue [*Creek*]. 2 full grown ones and 2 yearlings. Casper [*rancher Toles Cosper*] Said they was Some doing damage west of his place on his range.

[*Postmarked April 28, 1917.*]
Near Alpine Ariz Forks Blue River Millergans [*Milligan's*] Mill
Mr J. S. Ligon. Pradatory Animal Insp
                         Albuerque N M

Dear friend. Yours of March 24 at hand. I am always glad to hear from you. I recieved the pictures and am Very Thankful for them. They Represent the Situation all wright and I am Very willing to admit that I am the hardest looking animal in the Out fit. To use your expresion having the appearance of being found. I guess there is no one who Knows the Situation but what would willingly ad mit that I had been at least laying Out in the woods for at least 20 years continually. Yet not lost from my Self but comparitive lay lost to Others as it is hard to Know my where a bouts.

    I was Very mutch Surprised to find that the cattle & horse growers Assoation had had a meeting and failed to pay my claims. Mr McKeen Recommended the work and failed to Recommend the pay ment because he said it was in arizona. He told me they would pay for lions Killed in arizona if it was on the Members Ranges and that law was passed afer I had Killed the lions and they never notified me of the changes. I am writing Mr Miller the Secretary at Alborqueque a gain and then if He fails to pay I will have the matter taken up by a lawyer and report the transaction to the governor of the State. I will find out if they are allowed to make contracts and not live up to them. I did my part Just as I was In Structed to do and they have failed to do theirs.

    To Show you that I am not contrary with you I will take aneye Section you want me to work in for 3 or 4 weeks or a Shorter time and work the lions out for you at $50.00 per head all Sizes or I will work from 6 foot on up for $100.00. 6 ft down to 2 ft for $40.00. From 2 ft down $10.00. I Know of Several woolves that is Schattering a round in the Sections I am working in and it hardly looks like there is enough for you to Keep a man after. What will you give me for what I can get of them. So mutch for pups and So mutch for grown dogs and So mutch for bitches. There is no certainty when and how long I will work at a place as I am out for the highest dollar. No doubt you would not be in a Situation to consider Such propositions and yet you might feel interested in such conditions. Some times it happens that [I] find the wolves is only troubleing a part of the country I am getting bounty on and it would not be fair to tax them all for woolves. If you want me to I can Keep you posted as to where the woolves and lions and bear is doing damage and you can Send in your men. It will not enter fere with my business.

    I trailed an old She lion from the foot of the Blue range at head of Blue [*River*] to frisco [*San Francisco*] River range Near McKeefies [?] range. Dogs trailed all day and all night. Treed her at Sun up an old She. Had 4 Kittens in her about half grown. You can

Appendix A

See what a range they have and the damage a lion can do. I found a dead deer on the trail and where she had followed a mare and colt for miles and there was a full grown dead mare. When She treed the lion had been at the mare and I couldnt Say whether She Killed her or not as the dogs and lion tracks was boath there. I Saw where She Had Set at a deer lick for Some deer. The lick was under Some bluffs.

I did pretty well. I counted . . . [*illegible*] last month that I made $310.00 counting bounty and hides. That was a Kind of luckeye Strike and got full benifit . . . . Toar up 2 pair of overalls. Worked on Shoes every day. I expect to wind up this hunt in another week. Then I think I will Spend Some time collecting in the Eagle creak country.

I was Over at Mr. Pat McKeefies and Barnie McKeefies about the 12 of April. I was hunting that range when I went to move the little lion to washington for you and didnt get to work that Section only by chance as I took up work on the west Side of the Blue from Blue Po [*post office*] north to Millergans Mill and back east to the Peabelean [*Pueblo Creek?*]. I got after a lion on the Blue river and it trailed over on the McKeefie range and Killed it a 7 ft 6 inch Male and I trailed an old She and 2 yearlings for 2 days on the Sheep range and found where they had Killed Several Sheep. Then come a big Snow. In fact Snowed all day and the trails was entirely Snowed out. I was close to McKeefies camp. I went down and they paid me for Killing five big male lions on his range and wanted me to continue the work but Some of the Kelleys failed to pay their assesment and I disscontinued the hunt until it was paid. They have lost Very heaverly. More than they ever have before. I think that was caused by Mr McKeens range not being hunted and while I intended Keeping a close watch on that range moving the little lion Kept me out for a while and bad pay caused me to have to look up other work. I think from what I Saw they have lost about 60 Sheep from lions and cayouts and the bob cats is catching their lambs. Now they have put Poison on the range. Pat McKeefie is going on dickeyes Side and Said He would not put out aneye poison and asked me to Stay with him and He would pay me more moneye if I would Keep the work up. So I told Him that you would Send him a man in there that could Kill his Cayouties and Cats and Probaly get the lions. I gave Him your Address and Dr Fishers at Washington D.C. and Set down and wrote a Statement of how mutch Stock they were grazing and give as correct a Idia as to what they would nead as I could thinking that that would help you and Dr Fisher boath. I feal this way about it. They had room to complain and they neaded help and you would boath be willing to help them and no doubt doing So will Encourage your Industry. I guess you Know my Posture. I dont want to work for no Salereye. I did evereye thing I knew that I could do with the weather conditions and failed to give Satisfaction and I dont want a dollar that doesent belong to me and wont rob a man out of an hours time that Should be his. There is only one way to do a Strictly Concientiously buisness for me and that is to get pay for what I do. That is So mutch an animal. Lion hunting is too uncertain. Not long a go I had trailed a lion for 3 days and found he had went in a group of mts and I dicided that He was to far a head to over take Him but if I would wait 8 hours at that point and Stay there over night I had 2 places picked out that I might get his track fresh next morning by Stopping and if I hunted it that evening He might come in behind me and He would be lost. So I Stopped and by one hour next morning I Killed him. If I had been on Salereye I wouldnt lost that time but would have lost the lion.

I told Mr McKectheys [?] that I thought you were out on a trip and I didnt Know when you would be in as april is your best woolf month. One of the callars that was on your wolf chain was lost while it was at Mr Thompsons on blue River. The young man couldnt tell how it got lost. I sent you a big male lion hide Killed on grant creak. I am due you one lion hide and I agreed to kill it in this Section and charge no bounty for Same. So I guess I will Soon get it. I have Some Very Pretty hides on hand now and miself earned for. If you See aneyeone wanting Such things I can fill their orders.
Hoping to See you Soon

Yours Truly
B. V. Lilly
Blue Ariz

Appendix A

Letter to Ben Griffin

Fierro N.M. 8.4.1919. G.O.S. Ranch
Ben Griffin

Floyd La. Dear Ben

I am writing today to See if I can find you or hear from you. I dont think that I have heard from you Since 1904. I will try and get in touch with you through the mail.

I guess you Know your name Ben was named for me by your Father. Your Pa and [I] were on 2 or 3 bear chases to gather and He as well as myself always Enjoyed being to gather. I well remember your grand ma and your mother and her father and mother and all of the People are as fresh in my memory to day as the day I Saw them last all over West Carol Pa [*West Carroll Parish*].

I made a hunt in the Spring and fall of 1904 on Tensa [*Tensas*] river from its head to Fool River. I and the ones that happened to be out Some times with me Killed 28 bear. The ausford boys hunted Some that fall on fool River Sections. Cats woolves orters and Small game deer and turkey most any day. In the Spring of 1905 I went South down the Tensa Black River lower Miss. River and around Vermillion Bay Morgan City lower Chafalia [*Atchafalaya River*] and lower Red River. I got Some of most every thing. Bear pantha. I hunted on the gulf coast and Eilands. I hunted the gulf to west and East then Clear across the State of Texas. I Killed lots of Bear and all Kinds of animals in Southern Texas. I Shipped out 22 bear hides and 24 leopard cat [*ocelot?*] hides from 1 point at the mouth of Banard [*San Bernard*] and Brazos river and all Sorts of game and Sea fouls.

I worked west to rio grandy River west in to mexico at Eagle pass. Worked to Santarasa Mts. [*Sierra Santa Rosa in Coahuila*] then the Battle Began. Bear lions and all Kinds of wild animals. It was Kill and Skin. I would be out for 3 months See no one or even a track. I was collecting for the museum at washington D C. I got all Kinds of animals and fouls. I worked 7 months for a civil Engeneer Killing Deer turkey and bear for his camp meat. He ran 3 camps most of the time. I would Kill from 4 to 6 deer per day. Turkey and bear from 1 to [?] Bear a week. There was no other 4 men in the

Ben Lilly's Tales

Section that could Kill half enough meat to run them [*the camps*]. All of the hides was mine. Then I was paid a [*?*] to go in to Chawawa [*Chihuahua*] to Kill Some big grizzly Bear that was Killing men when they would camp out. I Sure worried thouh.

I have Killed lots of very large grizzly. I have a hide 12 ft long and 8 ft wide. I ask $500.00 dollars for it. I dont like to tell about these Big Successes when they are not Known. I followed that fellow 3 days in Snow from waist to Knee deep without a mouth ful to eat. Took me 3 days to get back and a month to get the hide out on act. of Snow. That was in white mountains arizona. I am now Killing mountain lions for the big ranches at $100.00 each. I got five last month. My work is at a Premium. I get just about 3 times as mutch as the best hunters get. I worked for the government 2 years of[*f*] and on and I Killed more Bears and lions than the 47 men they had working for them. I work in Ariz and N.M. I have Killed 227 Bear and lions in 7 years. 40 of these were bear. I can only Kill cow Killing bear big grizzlys. The government wants to protect them as a game animal.

There is lots of all Sorts of game where I am working now. The mountains is awful rough on the top of the ranges. Snow gets 10 feet deep in winter and Stays until April or later. I counted 33 deer in one bunch last winter. Blacktail. We have bouth white and blacktail also lots of antelope 3 Kinds of Bear Black Sinamon Brown and grizzly or Silvertip. I Shoot as well as ever. I never Saw a lion at aneye distance running that I didnt Kill. I have Shot maneye a cat at 400 yards full Speed. I always get led in them. I have Saw only 1 bear that I didnt led him. I Showed him to another man to Shoot and he didnt Shoot at all. Said He was to far. Lions is bad to Jump out [*when treed*]. I can usually at a distance of from 100 yards to 60 put 3 bullets in one before it hits the ground. I follow a bear or a lion Some times 3 to 6 days be fore I get to Kill them. The mountain lions Kills grown Saddle horses and grown cows. The grizly Kills all Sorts of cattle. This ranch [*the G.O.S.*] is about 40 miles nearly Square. I think they have over 7000 cattle.

[*Here parts of the letter are illegible.*] . . . with me . . . I have about 5 more [*dogs*]. I Keep them Scattered about to protect them from Hydraphobea or getting . . . . They are the finest trackers I have ever Saw. I often trail a lion until dark Saturday night lay over until monday ... [*then take*] the track and Kill him Monday or Tuesday. They [*the dogs*] loose it a heap but will work as long as I will let them. They are good bear dogs. I .... I toat an ax and build fires.

I worked in old mexico 3 years. In fact I have worked from the missisipi River to the pacific Slope and I Know more woods and mts than aneye man I have ever met and I am told that I am the most Successful big game hunter in the world and under Stand thier [*the animals'*] habits better and [*am*] the quickest Shot and I am equally good at extreme long range. My hounds is trained to Slow track. I raised and trained them all. I have 4 hounds that I ask $500.00 each. I raise one once and a while I have to Kill. I have 2 that Stayed 8 days with a lion and I Killed it. They will go to where a lion has Killed a cow or deer. After Staying treed a long time and eat then go back [*to*] the tree. That was taught them. If they are trailing and track is old I Stop them and feed and they go and pick up the track again So they have took up the Same habits.

If you can get hold of a march no. of the American magazine you will find an article and my picture and dogs and a live lion and a Skin of one just Killed. I got 36 letters in yesterday mail and a dozen or more writers from every Section is after pictures to get up articles and there is parties wants me to go out and chase down a lion or bear for pictures. I get $10.00 a day for Such efforts.

Write me as Soon as you get this. I want to make you Some Hunting Knives and Horns and hunting relics. Yours Truly B. V. Lilly

Letter to a Friend

Editor's note: Ben Lilly wrote this letter in 1924 to a friend who lived in Silver City. The man was probably a gun-shop owner, but this is not certain. In any case, Ben wanted the fellow to help him buy an army-surplus "trap door" Springfield rifle through the National Rifle Association. Prior to the tightening of the gun laws in the late 1960s, the N.R.A., with the approval of the federal government, sold obsolete military rifles and pistols to its members at low cost. Ben's letter is published here courtesy of the Silver City Museum.

Ben Lilly's Tales

◇ ◇ ◇ ◇ ◇

I want to buy a 45 70 Spring field rifle Single Shot with Long barrel and ram rod [*of*] steel. Can you get one from the Rifle asoiation [*National Rifle Association*] that has Spring [*set*] Trigger? I have for gotton what the moddle of the old Stile .45.70 is. The carbine is of same make [*and*] is moddle 1884. I want the long barrel with Steel ram Rod and Set Trigger if it can be found [*like*] new. I do not want and old rusty one or a Short one. You might inquire from the Am. R asoiation if they can fur nish me with what I want and the price of Same. Hoping to hear Soon yours Truly B V Lilly

Letter to J. B. Drake

Editor's note: The following letter, sent by Ben Lilly to an old friend in Louisiana, appeared in the July 26, 1928, issue of the *Morehouse Enterprise* newspaper published in the town of Bastrop. The note below was provided by the newspaper's editor.

◇ ◇ ◇ ◇ ◇

FAMOUS BIG GAME HUNTER RELATES HIS THRILLING EXPERIENCES

(Editor's Note—B. V. Lilly, famous big game hunter, and reputed to have killed more lions, bears and big game than any other hunter in the nation, has written a letter to his friend, Dr. J. B. Drake of Oak Grove. Ben Lilly is now located on a ranch in New Mexico. He is well known in Morehouse Parish where he resided many years, and old timers here will remember him. In his letter, which is very interesting, Lilly tells of his many experiences in hunting big game. Because of its unusual interest, and because it contains information of value, the Enterprise is publishing his letter in full, as received by Dr. Drake of Oak Grove.)

Appendix A

Fierro, N.M., March 12, 1928.
Mr. J. B. Drake,
Oak Grove, La.
My Dear Friend:

    I received your nice letter about two weeks ago. I had quite a spell of flu and was in bed for several days, it gave your letter a chance to catch up with me. Sometimes it takes three months for a letter to reach me, they will be forwarded to me from any point I have ever used as a post office and I have trouble in getting them, if they don't wear out before they reach me. I hope to get them in four months.

    My flu was caused from sleeping in a hotel at El Paso, Texas. I was called on to make a talk for the American National Live Stock Association. I went down and made them a 20 minute talk, and showed them over 200 pictures of wild animals and lions that I had caught, killed and tanned in camp. I also had pictures of 25 hounds, old and young that I have now at the G.O.S. Ranch. The short hand writers failed to catch the talk, they got so interested they lost out.

    You asked me how old I was, I was born in 1856. It may be I can cheer you up by telling you that in 1905 I was down on the Atchafalaya river, skinning bear I had killed and a young doctor stopped with me who was from Chicago, Ill. He said, that there was a man by the name of Henry Jenkins who died in lower California at the age of 169 years old. He was born in Yorkshire. His name was on record for 140 years. In January, 1919, I was near Chloride, N.M. and killed a very large lion and brought him in to the James boys' ranch to skin. The snow was three feet deep. There was a lot of books in the house and I was reading at night and found a little medical journal and in it I found Henry Jenkins history of his life, it told when he joined the oath of allegiance and stated that he left no track by which life could be prolonged. Mr. James gave me the little book, my daughter, Ada Mai has it. I sent it to her in 1919.

    Dr. Bebb was interested in the university at Chicago and sent out several pages of questions for Dr. Jessen to answer on the subject of dentistry and the general health of the human race and the causes of the many troubles that occur with mankind and the trouble that the wild animals have and the causes of them. They also give the birds and all of the fowls as a subject. Dr. Jessen was doing some work on my teeth and he asked me a few questions about the teeth and I answered them and he made the remark, "You are correct." He says to me, "There is not one man in a hundred that could have reasoned that out." As soon as he was through he asked me to look over the list of questions and see how many I could answer. I answered every one on the list, man, animal and birds. They were mailed to the university at Chicago. There was not a single answer turned down, it was stated, answered by B. V. Lilly. It was also stated that my answer had brought science and nature closer together than anything they had been able to get from any other man, and they regarded me the best naturalist in the field. They are trying to find the causes of diseases now and prevent them. They know how to doctor them, the thing is to prevent their developing.

I am sure you would be proud to know that my association and dealings with the Beouf river people has been very pleasant to think of, and many things that I know today that is valuable to me, was gathered in that locality. I have been blessed in my life, I feel interested in every thing that is intended for good. I have learned how to review life instead of worry. I can remember when I was a small boy and I go back to those days and bring up pleasant occurrences that took place in our father's and mother's family, and it renews life. I can't remember of my ever speaking a cross word to my brothers or sisters or to my father or mother. I am sure I never spoke a cross word to either of my children. I know they have never did anything that ever hurt my feelings, and I am as proud of them as I can be. My brother, Joe Lilly and wife is at Santa Rita, N.M., twenty-six miles south of this ranch. He was out to see me last Sunday. I am proud of all my old friends in every locality I have passed through. Well do I remember them all and in reviewing life I can recall every family that I have ever met and it is all pleasant for me to call over, no one but myself could imagine how kindly I have been treated in all sections I have traveled in the last 20 years, just a continuous journey in and through the wilds. I spent three years in Old Mexico and was treated so nicely and was a general favorite with every one I met. I have had the same friends abroad that I left at home.

This is March 25, it is impossible for me to get a chance to write. I have a nice little handmade knife I will send you as soon as I

Appendix A

get a chance. Dr. Jessen was down at my camp on a visit a few Sundays ago and they think Dr. William Bebb was caught in a snow storm and has perished. We have had several snows lately and it is cold and the wind very high. I am expecting to write a book soon, describing my life from boyhood to the present day, the localities I have seen, its soils and products, character of the waters, the health and its wealth and what each locality was noted for, the year I was in it. I will describe the soil, waters, elevation at the time I was passing, and I will describe the animals, domestic and wild birds, fish that has inhabited the different sections when I was there. I hope it will interest the younger ones as well as the few older ones, for it is claimed if I don't write it, it will be lost forever.

In the first place I have killed the largest and best tribes of animals. I was hunting so close that it will take them a long time to accumulate again as they was, it will take them longer to raise 100 under present conditions than it took me to kill 1000. No other man or men will work at it as close as I have. I have worked in localities that food could not be carried in sufficient quantities to keep three men alive, and I have worked where there was no water to be had for 76 hours, had neither water nor food in order to get the animals I wanted, and I succeeded. You can't find no one man that will take those chances not once. I have stayed in the snow for three weeks at a time and not even a blanket. I have followed big grizzly bears for three days at a time and not a mouthful to eat, snow from 3 to 12 feet deep, never had a coat on. I killed him, then I eat his meat. I am sure the hardships that it takes to make an equal with what I have accomplished, will never be carried out again by not even a dozen men. The more help they get the worse it will make it. No other man will try it alone.

The National Live Stock Association asked me to write an article for the Producer that is published at Denver, Colo., by the association, and I received a letter a few days since asking me to send them some of my pictures. I have over 100 pages written on the bear and lion, and also the panthers. I give their habits from birth to old age in every locality that I have hunted in. It tells of their killing people in the early days in Louisiana and Mississippi. The panther and mountain lion, cougar and pantara, puma and Mexico lion are one. American cougar is the scientific name for them, these other

Ben Lilly's Tales

names are what is called their common names where they are killed. If I kill one and send it to a museum I send the name it is called in the locality killed in and they send its scientific name back to me on their vouchers. I guess my old friend will be proud to know that the Illustrated World stated in January, 1920 that my record showed I had killed more bear and lions and had captured more live animals and had sent more to the museum.

Some of the men belonging to the Stock Association in the northern states wants me to take charge of a school to teach young men how to kill big game, and the animals that destroy live stock in the wild ranges where the domestic animals are being raised in the mountains.

I am today on the G.O.S. Ranch. It has 7,400 head of cattle and is about 60 miles one way, 50 the other and but one house located on it, that is the headquarters. It has a bunch of elk, more than 25 enclosed under a wire fence, over 200 turkeys turned loose on the range, the deer and wild turkeys are on all parts of the ranch. I killed 80 lions on it the first year I hunted on it and besides I killed lions and bears on other ranches adjoining it, and this year I only found two tracks of lions on the entire ranch.

I guess I could interest all of my old friends if I was with them, so you give my kindest regards to every one and you will not miss my good intentions. I thank you ever so much for writing to me. I will remember how you used to take so much pains in telling me things that I would ask you questions about. I have always regarded you as a wonderful man, strictly honest, truthful and Christian. You remember I often thought you and Sam Jones [*a prominent evangelist*] was alike, you are a natural teacher, yet you would never push yourself unless you saw it was appreciated.

My eyes are "A-1" yet. I improve in everything in my line except hearing, it is about the same, one ear is deaf. I am sure I improve in my shooting all of the time. If a bear or a lion ever jumps out of a tree and I am in sight, I will get three balls in it before it hits the ground. I never saw a lion that I didn't kill it or wound it so I could find it. I shoot well at ranges up to 400 yards, running or standing with a 30-30 or 33 or 303 calibre. I kill at long range by holding high over the animal.

Appendix B

LETTERS FROM BEN LILLY TO HIS DAUGHTERS

Editor's note: Ben loved his children, and after he left home they were always in his thoughts. He sent money to his wife, Mary, to help support the family when he could. However, maintaining a relationship with the children wasn't easy. Ben exchanged letters with his son and daughters after they were grown, and in late 1916 or early 1917 Hugh visited his father at the elder Lilly's camp near Alma, New Mexico (see Appendix C). Hugh Lilly suffered from tuberculosis, and sometime in the mid 1910s he moved to El Paso, Texas, hoping the desert climate would restore his health. The dry air and bright sun worked for some but didn't help Hugh, and he died in El Paso on January 2, 1918. There is no indication that Ben was present at his son's funeral, which was held in Louisiana.

It is doubtful that Ben saw his daughters after 1901. In August 1920 Ben visited his brother Joe in Mineral Wells, Texas, and sister Margaret Mills in Shreveport, Louisiana. But apparently he did not contact Ada Mai and Verna, even though they lived in the region. Verna Lilly (it seems she rarely used her first name, Beatrice) married Elmer Cecil Dodd in 1921; Ada Mai married Walter Bartlett "Bart" Eisely in 1924. It is quite certain that Ben did not attend his daughters' weddings. All this suggests that Ben discreetly avoided gatherings where his estranged wife, Mary, a "grass widow," might be present. Mary Sisson Lilly passed away in Brownsville, Texas, on January 27, 1931.[57]

Although they loved their "Papa," Ben's children undoubtedly had mixed feelings about their dad. That Ben's daughters were not particularly proud of their father is suggested by their reluctance to discuss him after his death. Frank Dobie was unable to obtain information from Ada Mai and Verna for his Ben Lilly book. Likewise, Monroe Goode was rebuffed when he contacted Ben's daughters seeking details about their father's life. In a 1945 article about Ben and his adventures Goode wrote: "It has been a real job to round up even part of the facts—Ben Lilly's children have been non-cooperative, which makes me wonder whether they have ever appreciated the heroic side of their father's nature." Both Ada Mai and Verna graduated from teacher's college, and Verna went on to earn bachelor's and master's degrees. It is understandable that these well-educated women might find their strange "mountain man" father something of an embarrassment.

Ben was in his seventies and living in New Mexico when he wrote the following letters. They were found among Verna Lilly Dodd's effects after her death in Monroe, Louisiana, in 1985. Fay Bowe, a Lilly relative who lives in Mer Rouge, Louisiana, donated copies of them to the Sandel Library at Northeast Louisiana University in Monroe, along with some photos, drawings, and other Ben Lilly memorabilia. They are published here courtesy of Fay Bowe and Northeast Louisiana University.

◇ ◇ ◇ ◇ ◇

Letter to Ben's Daughter Ada Mai
and Her Husband, Walter Bartlett Eisely

Mimbers [*Mimbres*] N.M. 8[9?].20.1929. at GOS Ranch

    Mr. and Mrs. W. B. Easley [*Eisely*]
    Tallulah. Louisiana.

My Dear Chicks. I think of you every day and yet I cant get a chance to write. I was Sending Some Knives out Some time a go and Sent 4 to you and Bart. They were not finished up. I wanted to make One for Mr. Dodds [*Elmer C. Dodd*] and one for Mr. Eisley So had Started 2 Small Iron handle Knives for you and Verner [*Verna*]. I threw in larger Sized Ones For them to Select from or describe what they would like to have me make for them. If they would mark off on a piece of paper what would Suit them I would be glad to do my Very best for them and it would be a pleasure to me to make Efforts in that direction. The ladies like the little Iron handle ones for

Appendix B

Kitchen use. I like them for camp or Skinning best. You can mak anye use of them that Suits and I will Take care of Each one the best I can. Each one discribe what they think they would want me to make for them. I have made Several Knives for the million aire [*probably William H. McFadden*]. They are proud of them because I made them and Say they cut better than Factory made Knives. It is So Stormy I can hardly hold the paper and cloudy and threatening rain. I Sent for handles but they failed to come.

I received Such a nice letter from Sister Sallie [*real name Sarah—Mrs. James H. Rogers*] after you and bart Visited Her [*in Hazlehurst, Mississippi*]. It made me so happy to Know you had Visited Her and Jimmy. I do wish Verner and Mr. Dodds could Visit them and Jiennie [*Jennie Lilly Franklin, a sister*]. Sallie thinks you are the Smartest Lilly of the Lilly Family. She is always partial to you. I guess Verna is Kept Very Busy or she would have wrote me. Even if we cant get time to write it makes us happy to think of Each other and I do feel proud of my chicks and all of my relations. It Seems that we have all been blessed and so energetic that we See So maneye People who fall down for want of energy. Sallie wrote me a nice letter discribing Magies [*Margaret Lilly Mills, another sister*] trip and margrets [*Margaret Mills, a niece*] and Said they intend to Visit you and that Her and Jimmy was going to Visit you and Bart.

Mr. & Mrs. [*Victor*] Culberson [*the owner of the G.O.S. Ranch and his wife*] is out yesterday and to day. We have lots of rain. Grass is fine. Roads impasable. Bridges washed out in places. The wind is so high now I cant Keep the paper down. The cow boys will all be in to night. Mrs. Mathews [*wife of John Mathews, the foreman of the G.O.S. Ranch*] and Every one is So nice to me. All treat me like a Brother.

Yesterday Evening I tried to finish this letter and a rain Storm came and decided that I couldnt write and the wind So high. I Soon Scratched out a big lion that I had Killed in old MEXICO. I managed to color him up in a way that He looked Very natural to me. I can make a Very good representation of aneye animal I Ever Killed. I never had a days instruction. I inherited that and the older I get the more natural it is for me to draw or Paint. I bought some water colors and a brush in Silver City 2 weeks ago. It comes natural for me to use the brush. Every Sunday evening I draw some little picture to remember How I use to get you and Hugh around me and I would Try to Teach you and Hugh how to draw. Each of you was Talented for that and was learning fast. Verner [*Verna*] was too Small to Start. Her talent was Inclined to exhibit things. She would go get little Kittens and bring them to me and Say look Papa they are pined to me. It was their Claws that was Sticking in Her little dress and I was Just as proud of Her as I could be. She would hunt up little chickens for me. You and Hugh would al ways gather a round me and get me to tell you about every thing that I Saw on my trips. That would interest each of you and Each one of you would Enjoy what I would Select to relate to you. Each of you could ask Very Inteligent questions on aneye Subject I would mention. I well remember I carried your mama and you and Hugh [*and*] Mr. Johnsons wife who was neighbor in Mer Rouge. We caught lots of fish on the east fork Bonidee [*Bonne Idee Bayou*] and had a big dinner and plenty fish to carry home. After dinner I fixed you and Hugh a Hook and pole. Each of you could catch more fish then aneye one in the crowd. You wasnt 3 years old if I remember wright. I have always thought that you three children had no equal for industry and behavior. I am Sure I never Spoke a cross word to either of you. Neither of you Ever hurt my feelings or Said aneye thing unkind to me.

This is Saturday Evening and I have Just been Touching up Some hand drawed pictures. Thought I might get them to you and Bart. And Venor [*Verna*] and Mr. Dood [*Dodd*] might come by and you could divide with them or they can tell me what Kind they like best and I will make them Some. It is a pleasure to me to draw for Each of you if you will Tell me what Each one would like to have. I want to make my Sisters all Some. It has rained Every evening for weeks. Threatened to day. I have paints. Has been too wet to use it.

I expect to Start out Monday on a hunt. I have every thing that I like to eat. Mrs. Mathews puts up nice lunch every day and I get all of the nice milk I can drink and I can always Kill the nicest of game when I am out. I would like to Visit you all but I am a fraid to go on the trains in Hot weather. I want to Start my book about the last of the fall months. Tell my 2 nice Soninlaws I am So anxious to See Them. I would be glad to Even have their Pictures. Have them taken with their wives. I am So proud of Them. I remember Bart [*as a little boy*] as well as can be. He looked cute and Seemed to be

Appendix B

interested in me and chatted with me a little. I hope you will ad mire the pictures. I could draw you one large enough to hang up in your Post office and they could See it without bothering you or bart. The People here are wild over them. One man ofered me 25 dollars to draw Him a grizly Bear. The People are wild for aneye thing they can get for a Keep Sake. Tell the little Billy Boy cat to Tel you to Let Him See the Lion picture and if He gets Scared He might not want to Sleep with me. Tell Him they are dead. Big rain coming and I will have to quit. Sister Sallie wrote me a nice letter and Sent your picture with billy Boy. It made me So happy to See your Picture. I am going to camp to day Sept. 13 1929.

Love to all Papa

Letter to Ben's Daughter Verna (Mrs. Elmer Cecil Dodd)

Mimbers [*Mimbres*]. NM. 6.24.1931. GOS Ranch

Mrs. E. C. Dodd
309 Ivy Street
Denton Texas

My Dear Daughter. I received a letter from Sister Sallie and She Said Our Ada Mai had wrote to Sallie Stating that She received a letter from you at noon and ada mai gave Sister Sallie your address and Ada mai had returned from New Orleans where She was attending a Teacher's meeting. She was representing the north Eastern part of Louisia. Ada mai mentioned that She Expected Elmer Carter [*Elma Carter, a female first cousin*] to come after Her in a Car and that She Expected to do Some planting in the Cemetary. I wrote Ada Mai and Sister Sallie and dark caught Me trying to draw in the dark for you. Hoping that I will get to see you and Mr. Dodd Soon and Ada Mai and Bart. Sallie asked me to arrang my trip to Suit you and ada mai and that would Suit best for all. I am Very anxious to See all of my Relations. I am Sure I will go wild over you and Ada Mai and I will be So glad to See Mr. Dodd and Bart. I Saw Bart in about 1905. He looked at me as Cute and was anxious to

Keep His Eyes on me. I remember him well. I will try to get this off tomorrow. I do wish you could have went to Mer Rouge with Elmer Carter and Ada Mai. The only thing to do is what we think is wright and abide by our own Judgment. I never feel the least uneasy about you or ada mai. You are Each So truthful and So Careful and So faithful that Each of you are as pure at heart and gods chosen Ones. Neither of my children never did or Said a thing that I could Ever ofer correction and on the other hand I was always Happy over their opinions about ocurances during Each day I Spent with them.

    This is the 26. Your letter did not get off yesterday. I wanted to use ink on the pencil writing for fear it could not be read easily. So I am mailing you Some pictures I drew thinking they would be Some company to you and Mr. Dodds. I make pictures on my Blowing horn of wild animals and they are So much company to me. I make camps in caves and under dry rocks and the little Wrens make nests and raise young under them for protection from the weather and I call all of the wren family Verner [*Verna*]. Named after you be cause you was the Baby in Our Family. You cant imagine how much Company to me. I name other things after Ada Mai and it is So Sweet to me to mention any of my familys names during the day or anye of my Fathers and Mothers familys names. The little Wrens comes at day break Every morning. Fly close to my head—I Say Verner Sweet little thing and I Saw one go out and brought back a bug and laid it down on a rock close to my head. That is did at different camps. They will have Some thing in their mouth and place it under a rock and come later and get it. Most of the wild fowls and animals get use to me and do not Shy me be cause [*I*] pay no attention to them. I found a Snake in my bed yesterday Evening. I let it Stay all night. Put out some water for it. I not much afraid of them. I have never been bit by one yet. I hope to hear from ada mai and Sister Sallie in a few days. It is So windy I cant half write. Kindest Love to All. Your devoted

        Papa

Appendix B

Letter to Ben's Daughters, Ada Mai and Verna, and Their Husbands, Walter Bartlett Eisely and Elmer Cecil Dodd

Mimbers [*Mimbres*]. NM July.11.1932. Mr. Tom OBrians [*O'Brien's*] Ranch

Mrs. and Mr. W. B. Eisely Tullulah [*Tallulah*] Louisiana
and Mrs. E. C. Dodds [*Dodd*] and Mr. E. C. Dodds

You Cant Imagine How happy I was to get Such a nice letter from Ada Mai and Her Picture. It looked So nice and Sweet and happy. I always realized that my chicks was the Sweetest things on earth and I was carried away with Ada Mais appearance. She looked as Happy as an Angel. I put it in the Bible and I would read the Bible and look at her picture and read again. So I Surely felt I was in good company. I do wish I could meet the 4 of you together at one time. I cant tell when I Can get to come to See the 4 of you. I think I may get to come over about September if I get a long well with my work. I am in hopes Vernor [*Verna*] and Mr. Dodds will Settle at Browns Vill [*Brownsville*] Texas. I think Talulah a nice place. I am pleased aneye where and I Know maneye localities. I was glad to hear of Ada Mai having so maneye pcts. I am Sure I was always happy when I could play with my chicks. We would have little plays and call Ada Mai Some Big Lady from New orleans and Vernor Some Big lady and Say She is from Some big town and Each one would Strut and feel big like a Lady grown. And Hu [*Hugh*] would act the Same way and I feel Sure those little plays was Interesting to me and your mother and no doubt was used as an assistance in getting by as Each one of you grew up older. Hugh Ada Mai and Verner would Each one Carry their parts in aneye play Suggested and I am Sure Each One of the 3 never Said or did one thing that could be classed wrong. And Just think what a pleasure it was for me to work and make money to asist Each of you if you Should happen to an accident. Each one of you proved to be a Success at your undertakings and Each one is as a Star in the Heavens to me. What a pleasure to my Heart and I have nothing but Hapyness to cheer my mind . . . [*The last part of this letter is missing.*]

Ben Lilly's Tales

Letter to Ben's Daughter Ada Mai
and Her Husband, Walter Bartlett Eisely
(Postmarked July 13, 1932)

Mimbers [*Mimbres, New Mexico*] Mail rout

Mr. and Mrs. W. B. Easley [*Eisely*]
Tallula [*Tallulah*] Louisiana

My Dear Chicks

I mailed Some painted Wild animals yesterday evening. They are for you and Bart and Verner [*Verna*] and Her Husband. So you and Venor Can davide them to Suit your Selves and when I come to See you all I can arrange grounds Rocks and mountain Senerie that will make them apear as they Should [*be*] arranged. I Sent them to California and they were Very Highly admired as a collection of wild animals that I had Killed all a lone in diferent Wild Locations and States. I have maneye more of all Kinds and maneye admireres. I may want to borrow yours and Vernors [*Verna's*] to place be fore the Chase [*a description of a hunt?*] in my Book So Kep them intil I recopie them. I [*have*] a fine bunch of Pictures that I Expect to Send to Mr. [*William H.*] McFadden as Soon as I Can find out where He is or where He would want them Sent. I am improving in my pictures. I can draw a large bear Mountain Lion or Deer Either in 10 minutes Time. Led pincil Sketch. And I can paint anye of the wild animals in 10 minutes large or Small Size. The pictures I have painted is the best I have Ever painted or Ever Saw painted [*and*] printed. I have learned how to make paints from Vegatables by boiling them down Very low and Save the Juce. I caught that by accident. It is getting Very cloudy and fixing for rain. It has been So windy that I could Hardly write or draw. I Cant Stay in a House and write or draw pictures. I have to be in an Opening. How is Mr. Dodds. Tell me what of a picture do you like best and what Size and color. I cant Say Just when I can come. I am well and Strong. I hunted in the Swamps west of Galveston on the west of Brasus [*Brazos*] River and on Boath Sides of the Banard [*San Bernard*] river from 40 to 60 miles up the River from the Coast and I hunted

Appendix B

West to the Colorado River [*in Texas*]. I really liked the Country from the mouth of Sabane [*Sabine*] river to Bay City and Still farther west. I Killed Manyi Bear and all Kinds of cats and Deer. No wild turkeys but Ducks and geese were plentyful and Deer. I was not at Brown Villi [*Brownsville*] Texas. I always thought I would like it. I crossed at Eagle pass when I went to Old mexico. I went over on the 8 of July 1908 and come out July 1912 [*actually about February 1911*]. I had a wonderful good hunt. I lived in the wildest places I could find and I was not sick a day. The GOS Ranch has had several buyers this month but no deal made yet. The Buyers are bothered about raising moneye that is out on notes. Mr. and Mrs. [*John*] Mathews [*the foreman of the G.O.S. Ranch and his wife*] is well and the Baby Jonnie Annie is Sweete pretty and Smart as a mouse. She Tries to be going Some where all of the time. She has nice buggys. She likes a horse. She is beautyful good natured and Happy and gets a long fine in Company. She is So Cute and real Smart. I have no time to write this morning on acount of having to catch the mail truck.

        Love to my
         Chicks
          Papa

        I will write you Soon

Letter to Ben's Daughters, Ada Mai and Verna, and Their Husbands, Walter Bartlett Eisely and Elmer Cecil Dodd

Mimbers [*Mimbres*]. N.M. Aug.3.1932 on Tom OBrians [O'Brien's] Ranch
Mrs. and Mr. W. B. Eisely Mrs. E. C. Dodds [*Dodd*] and Mr. E. C. Dodds

My Dear Chicks and Soninlaws Tallulah Louisiana

I am expecting a rain in a few minutes. We have had Several rains and Storms and crops is fairly good. Fruit crop was destroyed [*by*] freezing in Early Spring. I am Very anxious to See Each one of my chicks. Ada Mais picture is So much Company to me. I Keep it in my Little Bible that Sister Sallie gave me. I am So anxious to get Vernors [*Verna's*] picture. They will be nice company for me. On Sundays for me I read the bible and look at the Pictures I Keep in it. Write me if you can get a chance and we will Make it Suit for me to Visit Each one and Sister Magie and Sister Sallie and Jimmie and Sister Jennie. My Health is good. I have Several ofers from Others wanting me to write Articles on the Habits of wild animals.

> Kindest Love to All your devoted Papa
> [*Drawing of a honeybee*] V. Lilly

Appendix C

LETTERS WRITTEN BY BEN LILLY'S CHILDREN

Letter from Hugh Lilly to His Mother

Editor's note: Hugh Lilly was twenty-five years old and living in El Paso, Texas, when he wrote the following letter to his mother, Mary Sisson Lilly, who resided in Louisiana. Ben and Mary Lilly's only son worked at an ice plant, and he wrote the letter on company stationary. A consumptive, Hugh had relocated from Louisiana to West Texas for his health. The change in climate was not sufficient to combat the disease and the young bachelor died on January 2, 1918, one week after his twenty-sixth birthday. Hugh's letter is reproduced here courtesy of Delores Lomax of Longview, Texas.

◇ ◇ ◇ ◇ ◇

EL PASO ICE & REFRIGERATOR CO.
CAPITAL STOCK $100,000.00
PURE ICE & DISTILLED WATER
DAILY ICE CAPACITY 150 TONS
EL PASO, TEXAS

4/11-17

My dear Mother:—

I'll write you from the house tonight as it looks like when I am at the office I keep putting it off until two weeks have gone by since I wrote last. I expected to hear from you today, Wednesday but I guess I will get it tomorrow. I haven't any news to write about. I am still feeling fine as a new fiddle. We have had some mighty disagreeable weather lately. One day it would be like regular summer weather and the next as cold as winter. Tonight it has turned much colder and looks like we might have some rain or snow. Spring time in this country is far different than there. Here we have very little green stuff compared to the grass and trees there. The fall here is really the prettiest time of the year. I suppose that I think this because we always have the best weather [*then*].

I saw in the Mer Rouge paper where Mr. Spencer died and sent it on to papa. I was indeed sorry to hear of it. It looks like when it rains it pours. I think however most of it has been brought on by his extreme wickedness. You know when I met Mrs. Spencer and family in Nashville I thought then that they should stay up there [*away*] from their old associations for it seemed they were comfortably situated and should stay away from Mer Rouge inasmuch as their reputation was the least bit shady. I certainly sympathize with Merle and the other girl. I think Woodburn and Morrison are both about like the old man.

I wrote to Papa again the other day. I haven't heard from him in a long time but I still think he is around Alma [*a small town about sixty miles northwest of Silver City, New Mexico*]. Since being up there with him I can forgive him for being so irregular in writing for it is indeed a difficult job to write up there with his [*lack of*] conveniences for doing it.

Verna hasn't written me for some time. I think I shall surprise her tonight with a short note inasmuch as she has been so faithful in writing me.

How are Ada Mai and Aunt Annie Mai getting along with their civil service examinations? You write as if the burning of the Lilly mansion was a great loss. The joke tickles me. I realize the loss of an indifferent revenue from the rent amounts to a little but that's nothing to worry about. Don't worry over such trifles. Tell Jimmie to stick it out. He will come out all right if he just tries hard enough. I hope he is feeling better when this reaches you. Best wishes.

Lots of love—Hugh

Appendix C

Letter from Ada Mai Eisely to Miss Tirey

Editor's note: From about 1919 to 1925 Roy Tirey, his wife, Margaret, and daughter, Leolla, lived on the G.O.S. Ranch near Silver City, New Mexico. Roy was ranch foreman, and soon after arriving at the place he decided that lions were killing more than their share of G.O.S. cattle. He had heard that a hunter of considerable reputation named Ben Lilly was working near Blue, Arizona, so he sent a letter care of the Blue postmaster informing Ben that he was needed at the G.O.S. Several weeks passed, and one day Roy looked out the kitchen window and saw a bearded man coming up the road on foot with a long string of hounds trotting along behind him. It was Ben, and he soon taught the beef-eating lions the error of their ways. Lilly spent much of 1921-1922 guiding William Mcfadden and his party, then he returned to the G.O.S. as the outfit's resident lion and bear hunter.[58]

Leolla Tirey Duncan (born in December 1917) spent her early childhood on the G.O.S., and her parents allowed her visit Ben's camp near the ranch house whenever he was there. An only child, Leolla came to love the kindly and gentle old man and never tired of listening to his stories. Ben often shared his lunch with the little girl, a repast which usually consisted of nothing more than a bowl of cornmeal mush. Whenever Ben killed a lion or bear he gave Leolla a dime to celebrate the event. "Ben was my buddy," Leolla Tirey Duncan recalled in a recent telephone conversation with the editor.

The Tireys left the G.O.S. in the mid '20s, and in 1932 Ben moved from the G.O.S. to Tom O'Brien's ranch in the nearby Mimbres Valley. Early in 1933 the Tireys came upon Ben's camp on the bank of the Mimbres River. Ben was in a bad way and obviously couldn't live by himself any longer. Back home in Hanover, New Mexico, fifteen-year-old Leolla took it upon herself to write a letter to Ben's sister Sallie Rogers, who lived in Hazlehurst, Mississippi, explaining the old hunter's sad condition. Sallie forwarded the letter to Ben's daughter Ada Mai Eisely, and in response Ada Mai wrote a letter to Leolla, not knowing that she was just a schoolgirl.[59]

This correspondence resulted in Grant County officials being alerted to Ben's plight, and in the spring of 1933 they moved him from his Mimbres River camp to the county "poor farm." The rustic facility was located about fifty miles northwest of Silver City, on the north bank of Big Dry Creek. There elderly people in need were given food, shelter, and basic nursing care. The place was primitive by today's standards, but it was a great improvement over Ben's grimy campsite. The poor farm was run by Mrs. Mary Hines, a trained nurse, and even at the height of the Great Depression she never had more than about a dozen people to look after. There was a main building at the place, and there were some tiny cabins where the residents were housed. And it was a real farm—they grew their own vegetables, kept laying hens for eggs, had a milk cow or two, and raised a few pigs. Cal Salars, Mrs. Hines' nephew, visited the farm on several occasions when he was a boy (Cal was born in 1924). He remembers Ben as being pleasant and talkative but mentally confused. Now houndless and frail, Ben still yearned for the wilderness. Every now and then he would wander off, heading for the high country. Should Ben fail to show up for a meal, workers at the farm would track him down and bring him home.[60] Ben died at the poor farm on December 17, 1936. Ada Mai's letter to Leolla is reprinted here courtesy of Delores Lomax of Longview, Texas.

◇ ◇ ◇ ◇ ◇

Tallulah, Louisiana
Feb. 18, 1933

Miss Leolla Tirey
   Hanover
      New Mexico

Dear Miss Tirey,

    My Aunt, Mrs. Sallie Rogers, sent your very beautiful letter to me yesterday. Since reading the letter over and over I have tried to picture just what your role in life might be. At one reading I conclude that you are a nurse, another reading convinces me that you are a welfare worker, again you are a writer and later I think of you as a missionary. Whatever your station in life may be, you have truly served mankind by writing the very explicit truths regarding my very own father's condition.

Appendix C

To you, I am sure, I appear a most heartless creature to allow my father to suffer such pain by living a life of misery and neglect, but, really, I love him most devotedly and I have done everything in my power to get him to come make his home with my husband and me. He refuses to even answer my letters.

He has always lived in the style in which you find him living today. He refuses to live in a real house with people. The infirmities of old age have doubtless made his camp less sanitary than in former times. My heart aches when I think of the three comfortable beds in my home that are empty while he sleeps perhaps on a pile of straw, a worse bed than my dog sleeps on every night. We have thrown away food every day that he is dying for the lack of, no doubt. Oh! How I pray that he will some day see the folly of the chase and come to us.

If you see him anytime soon will you ask him, urge him, beseech him to come to us. I will gladly send him a ticket or if he cannot travel alone I will go for him. He has always had very biased notions about health conditions in the South, especially in our delta section. When you speak to him about coming, always refer to it as a <u>visit</u>, for if he thought he was coming home to die he would never come. He has always said that he wanted to die in the woods.

Years ago, before my brother's death, we became unduly alarmed about papa's existence. Our anxiety became so intense that my brother left for the wilds to search for him. He wired papa that he was on his way to see him. Papa did not want him to see what a miserable existence he was living so he wired my brother not to come, that he was going on a big hunt and would be gone for several months. Papa's brother had a similar experience when he tried to visit him. He has been a most devoted and indulgent father, but he tries to conceal from us the crude way in which he exists, like one concealing a bad habit.

You no doubt know papa and his peculiarities better than I. If you find that he will not consent to come to us but you can suggest a solution to this, my life's greatest problem, I shall be eternally grateful to you.

There are two of us—children to him in his day dreams. My sister, Verna, younger than I, who is in the University of Texas working on her Master's degree. Her husband is E. C. Dodd, dean of the Junior College in Brownsville, Texas. My husband is postmaster here and I am supervisor of the schools of this county. We do not want papa to suffer or die of neglect when we could easily take care of him, but he is very independent and will not accept anything that we try to do.

Please feel free to discuss this situation in its barest truth for I have a wild imagination and I always imagine the worst conditions existing. If papa ever realizes that we are trying to plan for him and his comfort, nothing less than a federal prison wall will keep him from leaping the bounds and going into the wilds never to return.

With a heart full of gratitude for your very kind interest in my poor old father, I am

                    Sincerely,
                    Ada Mai Eisely
                    (Mrs. W. B. Eisely)

Appendix D

A NEWSPAPER REPORTER INTERVIEWS BEN LILLY

Editor's note: Late in October 1922 William McFadden's two-year quest for a grizzly came to an end in Idaho and the members of his hunting party began to disperse. Ben Lilly had served as one of McFadden's hound experts and now, after six months in the Idaho wilderness, it was time to board a train and head for home. On his way to New Mexico Ben stopped in Denver for a day or two to see the great city of the central Rockies. A newspaper reporter in need of a story spotted a strange-looking character on the street, and it proved to be Ben. He then proceeded to interview the bearded houndsman. Ben obliged the man with a recounting of his life story, including his proudest moments as a hunter: his Louisiana bear hunt with Teddy Roosevelt in 1907 and the killing of the White Mountain grizzly in 1913. Now sixty-five years old and near the end of his hunting career, Ben still had grand dreams of future expeditions to far-off lands—Baja California, Alaska, Brazil. The old storyteller was in great form, and between Ben and his interviewer the facts took a beating. The article that resulted from Ben's encounter with the newspaperman, first published in the November 5, 1922, *Denver Post*, is reprinted here.

◇ ◇ ◇ ◇ ◇

Ben Lilly's Tales

VETERAN HUNTER OF BIG GAME HERE AFTER 54 YEARS ON TRAIL

Flowing Beard and Horn of Cow Needed Even in Denver, He Says.

By RAYMOND RICHARDS

Claiming practical purposes for both his rippling, spreading beard and the cow horn that hangs by a buckskin thong from his shoulder, Ben V. Lilly of the Great Outdoors is in Denver.

For fifty-four years Lilly has gone up and down the wildernesses of America, gaining the reputation which the late Theodore Roosevelt summarized when he said of him, "He is the best guide in the world on the big game trail, and one of the most intimately informed naturalists I have ever met." [*No source for this quote has been found. It is likely that Ben was just blowing his own horn a little.*]

Lilly's Denver visit is between two hunts. After while, by terms of contracts already signed, his hardship-toughened and weather-bronzed figure will head parties of wealthy sportsmen into the heart of the lower California peninsula, over barren Alaskan wastes and thru South American jungles.

And Lilly is 68 years old.

For two months, in the rugged region around Nampa, Idaho, he has been "puttin' thru a course of sprouts," a pack of thirty-five bear dogs of various breeds belonging to W. H. McFadden of Tulsa, Okla., a multi-millionaire oil operator and sportsman. The dogs are throroly trained now, and Lilly is on his way to the big "G.O.S." ranch near Silver City, N.M., where he proposes to institute fatal conditions for mountain lions that have been preying on cattle.

Training dogs and helping private ranchers and the government exterminate predatory animals are two of his specialties. Others are bear hunting for sport, game surveys, wild animal photography, and the expert collection of data and specimens for the Smithsonian

Appendix D

institute and other museums.

Born in the Mississippi wilds of 1854, forty miles from Jackson, Lilly contented himself with squirrels and rabbits until 14 years old.

"My gun was so long," said he, "and I was so short, that I'd drive a nail into a tree to rest the barrel on."

In his fourteenth year, he continued, he "prospected over into Louisiana and shot a bear, after which there weren't no holdin' me."

"Well, sir," he went on, "you might think it queer I wear this beard so thick, and tote this cow horn about these city streets. But one's just as needful to me as the other. Down in the Mississippi delta swamps, where I hunt a good deal, there's a powerful supply of poisonous bugs. I always sleep out on the ground, or on the rocks, or a log, and the heat of my body wakes them bugs up and starts 'em crawlin' and bitin'. I can fold my arms, and turn my coat up around the back of my neck, and pull my hat down and keep 'em off most of my face, and my beard protects the rest.

"And this horn, now. I got four dogs with me—crated up, poor pups. Suppose them dogs got loose at the depot, or the car turned over in a train wreck, which you never can tell about trains. Them dogs would get plumb away if I didn't have this horn—it's the only call they know."

National publications began to accord attention to the prowess of Lilly after he had won enthusiastic praise from President Roosevelt on a bear hunt in 1907 in northern Louisiana. The guide, hunter and naturalist is mentioned in several of the colonel's books. A recent issue of the Illustrated World said that, since 1904, Lilly has sent more valuable specimens of North American big game life to the Smithsonian institute than any other collector.

[*The brief (one page) article about Ben in the January 1920 issue of the* Illustrated World *makes no mention of the Smithsonian Institution or of the number of specimens Ben collected for the natural history museum there. Over the years Ben sent some 200 specimens (mostly large mammals) to the National Museum (see Appendix E).*]

Colonel Roosevelt bagged four bears [*actually one bear*] during the early [*October 1907*] Louisiana excursion, and the shout of "Bully!" was heard over the nation. It was with a warm letter of introduction from Roosevelt that Lilly went to Mexico, in 1908, to spend more than three years in Chihuahua, Sonora and other states, supplying surveying parties with fresh meat and finding "some mighty good huntin'." [*There is no evidence that Roosevelt had any contact with Lilly after the 1907 hunt, so the "letter of introduction" story is probably fiction.*]

"Now about this sleepin' on the ground that you folks seem to make so much fuss about," he said. "It doesn't seem unnatural to me. I haven't slept in a bed more'n a dozen times in twenty-two years, barrin' when I went travelin' acros several states like I am now—and layin' in a train berth can't properly be called sleepin'. I got a tent, but I don't use it much, because when I follow my dogs after a bear, we don't spend any time on good livin' and fol-de-rols. Get that bear, is our motto.

"If it's snowin', I sometimes set a big log afire at one end, and stretch out along the log near the fire. When it burns too close, I shift a little farther down the log. That's one system. Another is to get along without the log."

It was suggested that a log made a hard bed.

"No harder'n me," said Lilly. "I get my rest better on the ground than in a bed, anyhow. Why, I don't even miss not havin' a home, which I haven't since I sold my place in Mississippi in 1900. I'm goin' all the time, and I always walk when I can. Once—over in the White Mountains of Arizona this was—me and my dogs kept on the trail of a grizzly for three days without a mouthful to eat, but plenty of snow to tramp thru. When we got the grizzly we ate it. Shucks, that's nothin'."

Despite his disinclination as to beds, the picturesque veteran of the wilderness affects no dislike of cities.

"There's sure a lot to see when you get into one of 'em," he declared. "Trouble is, there's too much, and when I look, along comes a street car or an automobile, which keeps me jumpin' pretty lively, because one of my ears is bad—the left one. That doesn't bother me much in the mountains and woods—it kinda helps. I can't hear the dogs well from a distance, so I pick out a good one and tie him to me, and he follows the trail the pack takes, which gives me a chance to notice a lot of animal signs I wouldn't see on the short cuts I'd take if my hearin' was good."

Lilly expects to remain on the G.O.S. ranch until April. The Big

Appendix D

Grizzly country of Wyoming will claim him next for a bear hunt with R. L. Peddington, a rancher near the eastern boundary of the Yellowstone park. After that, his services will be required by McFadden of Oklahoma on a game survey and hunt in lower California, following which the wealthy sportsman will take him to Alaska.

"I hanker to try my hand on one of them polar bears," Lilly said. "I was told some time ago the grizzly I killed in Arizona was the biggest one mounted at the Smithsonian, and I reckon that means a polar bear is the only next biggest one there is. [*Ben's Arizona grizzly was not mounted for display. He sent the skull to the museum but not the hide. The bear's skull resides out of sight in a specimen cabinet.*] Then I've got arrangements made to go to Brazil with a crowd I've hunted with in this country. That'll just about round out my trainin' as a hunter, and it'll give me a chance to study the ways of a lot of animals I never met up with before." [*None of these trips to faraway locations took place. After 1922 Ben's hunting was restricted to southwestern New Mexico and southeastern Arizona.*]

Lilly was asked if he had ever thought, in his advancing years, of retiring.

"To what?" he asked.

Appendix E

ZOOLOGICAL SPECIMENS COLLECTED BY BEN LILLY

Editor's note: From 1904 to 1920 Ben Lilly sent approximately two hundred specimens of mammals to the U.S. National Museum in Washington. His collecting locales were: eastern and southern Louisiana (1904-1906), East and South Texas (1906-1908), northern Coahuila (1908-1910), northern Chihuahua (1910-1911), and southwestern New Mexico and Greenlee County in southeastern Arizona (1911-1920). A few of the animals he procured were smallish species, such as tree squirrels, but most were the larger species, including, of course, bears and mountain lions. It was beneath Ben's dignity to collect mice and other tiny critters. Ben killed most of the animals in this compilation, but he may well have acquired some of them from other hunters. Occasionally he sent in skulls he found in the woods. Many specimens consist of the skin and skull of the animal, but not a few are skulls with no skin and some are skins only. Ben occasionally sent specimens of birds to the museum, including two ivory-billed woodpeckers (now extinct) that he collected in southern Louisiana in 1906 and a spotted owl from Arizona's White Mountains (1914). But large mammals were his specialty. The following summary of his contributions is taken from a more detailed listing courtesy of Robert D. Fisher, Collections Manager of Mammals, National Museum of Natural History, Washington, D.C.

◇ ◇ ◇ ◇ ◇

Black Bear. *Louisiana:* 5 (Madison Parish, 4; Vermillion Parish, 1). *Texas:* 14 (near Kountze, Hardin Co., 4; near Bay City, Matagorda Co., 3; near Angleton, Brazoria Co., 7). *Coahuila:* 2 (25 miles NW of Múzquiz, 1; 160 miles NW of Múzquiz, 1). *Chihuahua:* 5 (San

Luis Mts., 5). *New Mexico:* 3 (20 miles NE of Monticello, Sierra Co. [Socorro Co.?], 1; near Magdalena, Socorro Co., 1; near Mimbres, 1). *Arizona:* 13 (near Blue, Greenlee Co., 13). *Total:* 42.

Grizzly Bear. *Chihuahua:* 1 (Mts. 11 miles W of Gallego, received in Washington Nov. 1910). *Arizona:* 2 (head of Horton Creek a few miles W of Blue, Greenlee Co., collected April 3, 1913, 1; near Blue, Greenlee Co., pick-up skull sent to Washington in 1915, 1). *Total:* 3.

Mountain Lion. *Louisiana:* 1 (12 miles SW of Vidalia, Concordia Parish). *Chihuahua:* 1 (near Gallego, collected Nov. 1910). *New Mexico:* 16 (near Socorro, 3; near Reserve, 6; 15 miles N of Alma, 4; near Chloride, 2; near Mimbres, 1). *Arizona:* 24 (near Blue, Greenlee Co., 16; near Clifton, Greenlee Co., 8). *Total:* 42.

Ocelot. *Texas:* 4 (18 miles NW of Angleton, 3; 18 miles E of Bay City, 1). *Total:* 4.

Bobcat. *Louisiana:* 12 (near Tallulah, 6; mouth of Fool River, 1; 15 miles W of Vidalia, 2; near Abbeville, 1; near Plaquemine, 1; near Lake Charles, 1). *Texas:* 3 (near Kountze, Hardin Co., 1; 19 miles NW of Angleton, Brazoria Co., 2). *Total:* 15.

Feral House Cat. *Louisiana:* 1 (near Abbeville). *Total:* 1.

Lobo Wolf. *Chihuahua:* 1 (collected Nov. 1910 near Gallego). *NW Chihuahua or SW New Mexico:* 2 (recieved Feb. 25, 1911, precise collection localities unknown, 2). *Total:* 3.

Red Wolf. *Louisiana:* 7 (near Tallulah, 3; Indian Lake 23 miles SW of Tallulah, 1; near Floyd, 1; Macks Bayou 3 miles E of Tensas River, Madison Parish, 1; 20 miles SW of Vidalia, 1). *Texas:* 1 (near Kountze). *Total:* 8.

Coyote. *Coahuila:* 2 (25 miles NW of Múzquiz, 1; 110 miles NW of Múzquiz, 1). *Total:* 2.

Ben Lilly's Tales

Gray Fox. *Coahuila:* 2 (Hacienda de la Palma near Múzquiz, 1; Burro Canyon 140 miles NW of Múzquiz, 1). *Total:* 2.

Raccoon. *Louisiana:* 14 (near Tallulah, Madison Parish, 3; near Lake Ridge 5 miles SE of Fool River, 1; near Abbeville, Vermillion Parish, 10). *Texas:* 2 (near Kountze, Hardin Co., 1; near Angleton, Brazoria Co., 1). *Coahuila:* 1 (Mariposa Ranch 36 miles NW of Múzquiz). *Total:* 17.

Ringtail. *Coahuila:* 1 (25 miles NW of Múzquiz). *Total:* 1.

Striped Skunk. *Louisiana:* 3 (near Abbeville, 3). *Total:* 3.

River Otter. *Louisiana:* 3 (Bear Lake 8 miles W of Tallulah, 2; 12 miles SW of Tallulah, 1). *Texas:* 4 (18 miles E of Bay City, 1; 20 miles W of Angleton, Brazoria Co., 3). *Total:* 7.

White-tailed Deer. *Louisiana:* 24 (East Carroll Parish, 3; near Tallulah, 5; near mouth of Fool River, 3; near Indian Lake, 1; near Lake Providence, 1; near Bear lake, 1; near Rayville, 1; near Abbeville, 7; Price Island, 1; near Schooner Bayou, 1). *Texas:* 5 (near Kountze, 2; near Bay City, 2; near Angleton 1). *Coahuila:* 2 (Mariposa Ranch 36 miles NW of Múzquiz, 2). *Total:* 31.

Mule Deer. *Coahuila:* 1 (Talbolocis Ranch 180 miles NW of Múzquiz). *Total:* 1.

Virginia Opossum. *Louisiana:* 1 (20 miles S of Abbeville). *Total:* 1.

Rafinesque's Big-eared Bat. *Louisiana:* 2 (near Tallulah, 2). *Total:* 2.

Muskrat. *Louisiana:* 5 (20 miles SW of Abbeville, 5). *Total:* 5.

Black-tailed Jack Rabbit. *Coahuila:* 2 (Piedra Blanca Ranch 140 miles NW of Múzquiz, 2). *Total:* 2.

Appendix E

Desert Cottontail. *Coahuila:* 1 (Piedra Blanca Ranch 140 miles NW of Múzquiz). *Total:* 1.

Gray Squirrel. *Texas:* 1 (near Kountze, Hardin Co.). *Total:* 1.

Fox Squirrel. *Texas:* 2 (Sabine River 30 miles S of Newton, 2). *Total:* 2.

Eastern Woodrat. *Louisiana:* 2 (near Franklin, 2). *Texas:* 2 (near Kountze, 2). *Total:* 4.

Plains Pocket Gopher. *Texas:* 2 (Sabine River 30 miles S of Newton, 2). *Total:* 2.

CITATIONS

1. Bowe 1997; White 1994.
2. Roosevelt 1919, pp. 209-210.
3. Malone 1935.
4. Fisher 1997; Appendix E.
5. Fisher 1997; Appendix E.
6. Cameron 1929, pp. 275-276.
7. Ligon 1974. See also Appendix A, "Letter to A. K. Fisher."
8. Goode 1945; Dobie 1950, p. 167.
9. Dobie 1950, pp. 127-128, 167.
10. Peoples 1978.
11. Duncan 1998; Collyge 1998; Shannon 1992; Appendix C, "Letter to Miss Tirey."
12. Anon. 1936; Bowe 1997; Duncan 1998; Appendix C.
13. Hoffmeister 1986, p. 484.
14. Brown 1985, pp. 61-65.
15. Hilliard 1996, pp. 10-18, 152.
16. Vernon Bailey (1931, p. 361) was the first to erroneously assert that Lilly's "three-state" bear was a grizzly. Relying upon Bailey, subsequent authors have repeated this mistake.
17. Fisher 1998.
18. Housholder 1961, October, p. 23; Housholder 1971, p. 32; Hoffmeister 1986, p. 480. Bob Housholder, an outdoor writer and the source of mammalogist Donald Hoffmeister's version of the fictitious 500-mile grizzly chase, reported (1961) that he got the story from Dr. Frank C. Hibben of the University of New Mexico.
19. Brown 1985, pp. 81, 151-165.
20. Hansen 1992, pp. 9-14; Logan and others 1996, pp. 43, 59, 142.
21. Poole and Schantz 1942, p. 87; Fisher 1997.
22. Fisher 1997.
23. Brown 1985, p. 65.
24. Schullery 1992, p. 42.

Citations

25. Brown and Carmony 1990, pp. 152-154; Pearce 1965, p. 88; U.S. Forest Service map "Gila National Forest."
26.. Hansen 1992, p. 13.
27. Logan and others 1996, p. 42.
28. Schullery 1992, pp. 28, 35, 63; Brown 1985, p. 74.
29. Hansen 1992, pp. 12, 24; Logan and others 1996, pp. 144, 150; Shaw 1987, pp. 16-17.
30. Hansen 1992, pp. 24-27; Logan and others 1996, p. 150.
31. Hansen 1992, pp. 16-17, 25; Logan and others 1996, pp. 46-49, 62, 141-142.
32. Hansen 1992, pp. 13-14; Logan and others 1996, pp. 43, 59.
33. Hansen 1992, pp. 13-14; Logan and others 1996, pp. 42-44, 57, 59.
34. Hansen 1992, p. 10; Logan and others 1996, p. 142.
35. Hansen 1992, pp. 11, 24, 27; Logan and others 1996, pp. 142, 150.
36. Hansen 1992, p. 9.
37. Hansen 1992, pp. 38-39.
38. Hansen 1992, pp. 12-14, 16-17, 24-27; Logan and others 1996, pp. 46-48, 62, 141-142, 150, 200-201, 206.
39. Hansen 1992, p. 9-11; Logan and others 1996, pp. 43, 49, 59, 142.
40. Schullery 1992, pp. 26, 64.
41. Schullery 1992, pp. 17-22, 57-61.
42. Schullery 1992, p. 42.
43. Schullery 1992, pp. 26, 64.
44. Brown 1985, pp. 11-12.
45. Ligon 1974; Appendix A, "Letter to A. K. Fisher."
46. Goode 1945; Dobie 1950, p. 167.
47. Hansen 1992, pp. 12, 24-27; Logan and others 1996, pp. 144, 150; Shaw 1987, pp. 16-17.
48. Hansen 1992, pp. 24-27; Logan and others 1996, p. 150.
49. Goode 1945.
50. Dobie 1950, pp. 154-157.
51. Salmon 1991, p. 49.
52. LeCount 1986, pp. 4-6.
53. Hibben 1950, pp. 109-132.
54. Fisher 1997.

Ben Lilly's Tales

55. Goode 1945; Cooley 1947; Dobie 1950, p. 218.
56. White 1997; Lomax 1997.
57. Bowe 1997; Peoples 1978.
58. Collyge 1998.
59. Duncan 1998; Shannon 1992.
60. Salars 1998.

SOURCES AND REFERENCES

Anon. 1920. "Hunting Lions in the U.S. Is His Long Suit." *Illustrated World*, Vol. XXXII, No. 5 (January), p. 706.

_____. 1928. "New Mexico Trapper Entertains Delegates with Tales of Big Game Hunting on Cattle Ranges." *El Paso Times*, January 26. (Describes Ben Lilly's talk at the American National Livestock Association convention.)

_____. 1936. "Ben Lilly is Dead." *Silver City Enterprise*, December 18.

_____. 1936. "Famous Trapper and Hunter Laid to Rest: Relatives Here for Funeral Held Monday." *Silver City Enterprise*, December 25.

_____. 1956. "W. H. McFadden, Fabled Oil Pioneer, Dies in Fort Worth." *The Ponca City News*, November 2. (This obituary includes an interesting biographical sketch of McFadden.)

Bailey, Vernon. 1931. *Mammals of New Mexico*. North American Fauna No. 53. U.S.D.A. Bureau of Biological Survey, Washington, D.C. (Bailey discusses Lilly's "three state" bear, killed in 1911 in Chihuahua near the New Mexico line, on page 361. He erroneously classified the bear as a grizzly.)

Baker, Robert D., and others. 1988. *Timeless Heritage: A History of the Forest Service in the Southwest*. FS-409. U.S.D.A Forest Service.

Bowe, Fay. 1997. "Personal communications with Neil Carmony regarding Ben Lilly and his family." (Fay Bowe of Mer Rouge, Louisiana, is a Lilly relative and has researched the family extensively.)

Brown, David E., ed. 1983. *The Wolf in the Southwest: The Making of an Endangered Species*. University of Arizona Press, Tucson. (Includes information on J. Stokley Ligon and the Biological Survey's predator eradication programs in Arizona and New Mexico.)

Brown, David E. 1985. *The Grizzly in the Southwest: Documentary of an Extinction*. University of Oklahoma Press, Norman. (Includes a biographical sketch of Ben Lilly on pages 177-188. Reprinted in 1996 with a new foreword and preface.)

Brown, David E., and John A. Murray, eds. 1988. *The Last Grizzly and Other Southwestern Bear Stories*. University of Arizona Press, Tucson. (A story by Ben Lilly and one about him are reproduced on pages 92-100.)

Brown, David E., and Neil B. Carmony, eds. 1990. *Aldo Leopold's Wilderness*. Reprint: University of New Mexico Press, Albuquerque, 1995 (under the title *Aldo Leopold's Southwest*).

Burk, Dale, ed. 1979. *The Black Bear in Modern North America*. Boone and Crockett Club and The Amwell Press, Clinton, New Jersey.

Burridge, Gaston. 1952. "Ben Lilly, Last of the Mountain Men." *Arizona Wildlife-Sportsman*, Vol. 23, No. 5 (May), pp. 20-24, 64-67.

———. 1953. "Lilly Makes a Knife." *Arizona Wildlife-Sportsman* Vol. 24, No. 4 (April), pp. 12-16.

———. 1954. "Lilly's Big Grizzly." *Arizona Wildlife-Sportsman* Vol. 25, No. 1 (January), pp. 16-17, 60-62.

Cameron, Jenks. 1929. *The Bureau of Biological Survey: Its History, Activities and Organization*. Institute for Government Research (Brookings Institution) Service Monographs of the United States Government No. 54. Johns Hopkins Press, Baltimore.

Carmony, Neil B. 1995. "Some Lee Family History." In: *Onza! The Hunt for a Legendary Cat*. High-Lonesome Books, Silver City, New Mexico, pp. 62-104. (Biographical material on hound man Dale Lee and his brothers.)

Collyge, Billy Joe. 1998. "Personal communications with Neil Carmony regarding Roy Tirey, foreman of the G.O.S. Ranch during the early 1920s." (Billy Joe Collyge of Silver City, New Mexico, knew Roy and Margaret Tirey well during their retirement years and spoke with them often about Ben Lilly. The Tireys are now deceased.)

Cooley, Hal. 1947. "Memorial Plaque Will Honor Memory and Hunting Legends of Ben V. Lilly." *Silver City Daily Press*, June 17.

Coor, Cleo Cosper, ed. 1987. *Down on the Blue: Blue River, Arizona, 1878-1986*. Privately published by the Blue River Cowbelles. (Includes information on Toles Cosper and many other Blue River ranchers.)

Craighead, Frank C., Jr. 1979. *Track of the Grizzly*. Sierra Club Books, San Francisco.

Cunningham, Stanley C., and others. 1995. *Evaluation of the Interaction Between Mountain Lions and Cattle in the Aravaipa-Klondike Area of Southeast Arizona*. Research Branch Technical

Report No. 17. Arizona Game and Fish Department, Phoenix.

Dobie, J. Frank. 1943. "Ben Lilly of the Mountain." Reprinted in: *Afield with J. Frank Dobie: Tales of Critters, Campfires, and the Hunting Trail.* Edited by Neil B. Carmony. High-Lonesome Books, Silver City, New Mexico, 1992, pp. 71-85. (First published in the September-October 1943 issue of *Arizona Highways*.)

_____. 1950. *The Ben Lilly Legend.* Little, Brown and Company, Boston.

Duncan, Leolla Tirey. 1998. "Personal Communications with Neil Carmony regarding her memories of Ben lilly." (In the early 1920s, Mrs. Duncan, then a young girl, lived on the G.O.S. Ranch where Ben had his main camp and came to know him well. Mrs. Duncan now lives in Clovis, California.)

Evans, G. W. "Dub." 1951. *Slash Ranch Hounds.* University of New Mexico Press, Albuquerque.

Findley, James S., and others. 1975. *Mammals of New Mexico.* University of New Mexico Press, Albuquerque.

Fisher, Robert D. 1997. "Personal communications with Neil Carmony regarding grizzly bears specimens collected by B. V. Lilly." (According to Robert Fisher, Collections Manager of Mammals, National Museum of Natural History, Biological Resources Division, U.S.G.S., Washington, D.C., the National Museum houses three grizzly bear skulls sent in by Ben Lilly: 1. USNM No. 170557. Male, shipped from Gallego, Chihuahua, and received November 1910. Museum records indicate that the bear was killed eleven miles west of Gallego. No skin. 2. USNM No. 212436. Male, killed near Horton Creek, White Mountains, Arizona, April 3, 1913. No skin. The skull is 375 mm (14.8 in.) in overall length has a bullet hole in it. 3. USNM No. 206451. Skull received in 1915. Collected near Blue, Arizona. No skin. Sex not indicated. Weathered and undoubtedly a "pick-up" specimen. It is doubtful that Lilly killed any grizzlies other than the first two bears listed above, and one of them, the Gallego bear, was probably shot by Frank Sanborn, a sportsman guided by Lilly. The animals were scarce when Ben arrived in the Southwest, and the National Museum was eager to buy grizzly skulls. It would be odd for Ben, a very frugal man, to throw away something he could readily sell.)

_____. 1998. "Personal communications with Neil Carmony regarding the mammal specimens Ben Lilly sent to the U.S. National Museum." (From 1904 to 1920 Lilly sent approximately 200 specimens to the National Museum in Washington, D.C.)

Fuehr, Irma. 1943. "The Lilly Legend." *New Mexico*, January, pp. 10, 30-31.

Goode, Monroe H. 1945. "Ben V. Lilly." *The Cattleman*, Vol. 31, No. 10 (March), pp. 31-32, 125-127; Vol. 31, No. 11 (April), pp. 15-17, 52.

Guthrie, John D. 1938. "More About Ben Lilly." *American Forests*, Vol. 44, No. 9 (September), p. 386. (Letter to the magazine's editor.)

Hansen, Kevin. 1992. *Cougar, the American Lion.* Northland Publishing, Flagstaff, Arizona. (A comprehensive summary of the results of modern mountain lion research.)

Hawley, Jesse E. 1998. "Personal communications with Neil Carmony regarding Ben Lilly." (J. E. Hawley, who now lives in Phoenix, Arizona, was still vigorous in March 1998 at the age of ninety. He met Lilly only one time, in the fall of 1926. Hawley was nineteen, and he and his boss, government hunter Albert Pickens, spent a quiet Sunday at Ben's camp in the mountains east of Buckhorn, New Mexico. See Sweet 1998.)

Hibben, Frank C. 1948. "Last of the Mountain Men." *Outdoor Life*, May, pp. 47-53. (Reprinted as chapter one, "Ben Lilly," in *Hunting American Lions*—see below.)

_____. 1948. *Hunting American Lions.* Reprint: High-Lonesome Books, Silver City, New Mexico, 1995.

_____. 1950. *Hunting American Bears.* Reprint: High-Lonesome Books, Silver City, New Mexico, 1996. (The 1996 edition includes two chapters on Ben Lilly and a letter from Lilly to Washington bureaucrat A. K. Fisher as an appendix.)

Hilliard, George. 1996. *A Hundred Years of Horse Tracks: The Story of the Gray Ranch.* High-Lonesome Books, Silver City, New Mexico.

Hoffmeister, Donald F. 1986. *Mammals of Arizona.* Arizona Game and Fish Department, Phoenix, and the University of Arizona Press, Tucson.

Hoover, H. A. 1958. *Tales from the Bloated Goat: Early Days in Mogollon.* Reprint: High-Lonesome Books, San Lorenzo, New Mexico, no date.

Housholder, Bob. 1961. "The Grizzly Bear In Arizona." A four-part article that appeared in the July (Vol. 32, No. 7, pp. 16-19, 57-58), August (Vol. 32, No. 8, pp. 14-16, 52), September (Vol. 32, No. 9, pp. 14-16), and October (Vol. 32, No. 10, pp. 23-26, 34) issues of *Arizona Wildlife-Sportsman* magazine.

_____. 1971. *The Grizzly Bear in Arizona.* Second edition. Privately published by the author. (Much of this material first appeared in 1961 in *Arizona Wildlife-Sportsman* magazine.)

Jackson, David G. 1961. "Requiem for a Pioneer: The Story of J. Stokley Ligon." *New Mexico Wildlife*, May-June, pp. 4-6.

James, Edward T., ed. 1973. *Dictionary of American Biography, Supplement Three, 1941-1945.* "Marland, Ernest Whitworth (May 8, 1874—Oct. 3, 1941)." Charles Scribner's Sons, New York, pp. 504-506. (Marland was W. H. McFadden's partner in the oil business.)

Jones, P. J. 1997. "Mer Rouge Monument Will Honor Ben Lilly." *The Bastrop (La.) Daily Enterprise*, February 27.

Kiene, L. L. 1967. "Texas Bear Hunt, 1906." In: *Tales from the Big Thicket.* Edited by Francis E. Abernathy. University of Texas Press, Austin, pp. 123-136. (First Published in the *Topeka State Journal* in December 1906.)

LeCount, Albert L. 1986. *Black Bear Field Guide: A Manager's Manual.* Special Report No. 16. Arizona Game and Fish Department, Phoenix.

Lee, Dale. 1981. *Life of the Greatest Guide: Hound Stories and Others of Dale Lee.* Edited by Robert McCurdy. Privately published by the editor.

_____. 1982. *Greatest Hound Stories Ever Told.* Recorded by Claude Miller, Springdale, Arkansas. (Twenty audio cassettes featuring Dale Lee recounting his hunting adventures. His comments about Ben Lilly are on cassette number two.)

Leopold, A. Starker. 1959. *Wildlife of Mexico: The Game Birds and Mammals.* University of California Press, Berkeley.

Ligon, J. Stokley. 1916. "Inspector's Annual Report, Predatory Animal Control, Arizona and New Mexico, Fiscal Year July 1, 1915, to June 30, 1916." U.S.D.A Bureau of Biological Survey, Albuquerque, New Mexico, August 25.

_____. 1917. "Annual Report of Inspector, Predatory Animal Control, Arizona and New Mexico, July 1, 1916, to June 30, 1917." U.S.D.A. Bureau of Biological Survey, Albuquerque, New Mexico, August 28.

_____. 1918. "Annual Report, Predatory Animal Campaign, Arizona—New Mexico, July 1st, 1917, to June 30th, 1918." U.S.D.A. Bureau of Biological Survey, Albuquerque, New Mexico.

_____. 1927. *Wild Life of New Mexico: Its Conservation and*

Management. New Mexico State Game Commission, Department of Game and Fish, Santa Fe.

_____. 1974. "Hiring Ben Lilly for the Biological Survey." In: *Wilderness of the Gila*. Edited by Elizabeth Fleming McFarland. Crest Press, Silver City, New Mexico, pp. 40-43. (McFarland did not identify the source of this article. It may have been transcribed from audio tapes of old-timers' stories recorded by Louis Blachly. J. S. Ligon died in 1961 at the age of 81.)

Lilly, Benjamin V. "File." Special Collections Department, Sandel Library, Northeast Louisiana University, Monroe. (Includes letters Ben Lilly wrote to his daughters and some family photos. Most of this material came from the estate of Verna Lilly Dodd (1897-1985) courtesy of Fay Bowe of Mer Rouge, Louisiana.)

_____. "File." Silver City Museum, Silver City, New Mexico. (The museum houses several Ben Lilly photos, a copy of Ben's manuscript on lions and bears, several Lilly letters, and numerous articles about Ben from newspapers and magazines.)

_____. 1916. "Dr. A. K. Fisher. Dear Friend . . ." In: *Hunting American Bears* by Frank C. Hibben. High-Lonesome Books, Silver City, New Mexico, 1996 (reprint edition), pp. 263-265. (This letter, dated April 21, 1916, was mailed from Clifton, Arizona, and received at the Washington, D.C., office of the Biological Survey on April 28. Albert Fisher was a senior Biological Survey official.)

_____. 1916. "Mountain Lion Kill Record." Typed copy in editor's files. Also in the Ben Lilly file, Silver City Museum, and the J. Frank Dobie Collection, Harry Ransom Humanities Research Center, University of Texas at Austin.

_____. 1922. "Idaho Hunting Diary." Typed copy in editor's files. Also in the Ben Lilly file, Silver City Museum, and the J. Frank Dobie Collection, Harry Ransom Humanities Research Center, University of Texas at Austin.

_____. Ca. 1920s. "Mountain Lions of New Mexico." Copy of typescript in editor's files. Also in the Ben Lilly file, Silver City Museum, and the J. Frank Dobie Collection, Harry Ransom Humanities Research Center, University of Texas at Austin.

_____. Ca. 1920s. "Bears of Arizona and New Mexico." Copy of typescript in editor's files. Also in the Ben Lilly file, Silver City Museum, and the J. Frank Dobie Collection, Harry Ransom Humanities Research Center, University of Texas at Austin.

_____. 1928. "Famous Big Game Hunter Relates His Thrilling Experiences." *Morehouse Enterprise* (Bastrop, Louisiana), July

26. (Letter from B. V. Lilly to J. B. Drake dated March 12, 1928.)

_____. 1928. "Bears and Lions." *The Producer*, Vol. 10, No. 2 (July), pp. 3-6; Vol. 10, No. 3 (August), pp. 3-7.

Logan, Kenneth A., and others. 1996. *Cougars of the San Andres Mountains, New Mexico.* Hornocker Wildlife Institute, University of Idaho, Moscow, and New Mexico Department of Game and Fish, Santa Fe. (The results of a ten-year study, the most comprehensive by far of any conducted in the region, are presented in this 280-page report.)

Lomax, Delores. 1997. "Personal communications with Neil Carmony regarding Ben Lilly and his family." (Mrs. Lomax's late husband, Bob Lomax (1911-1996), was a Lilly relative, and he researched Ben Lilly and his family extensively. Mrs. Lomax lives in Longview, Texas, and shares her husband's interest in Ben Lilly.)

McFarland, Elizabeth Fleming, ed. 1974. *Wilderness of the Gila.* Crest Press, Silver City, New Mexico.

McLean, Mickey. 1996. "Ben Lilly's Legend in Parish Continues Today." *The Bastrop (La.) Daily Enterprise*, February 29.

Malone, Dumas, ed. 1964. *Dictionary of American Biography, Volume IX, Part II.* "Talmage, Thomas DeWitt (January 7, 1832—April 12, 1902)." Charles Scribner's Sons, New York, pp. 287-288.

Merriam, C. Hart. 1916. "Nineteen Apparently New Grizzly and Brown Bears from Western America." *Proceedings of the Biological Society of Washington*, Vol. 29, pp. 133-154.

_____. 1918. *Review of the Grizzly and Big Brown Bears of North America (Genus Ursus)* . . . North American Fauna No. 41. U.S.D.A. Bureau of Biological Survey, Washington, D.C. (In this work, now dismissed by mammalogists as hopelessly flawed, Merriam described seventy-eight species of grizzly bears. Lilly's White Mountains, Arizona, grizzly, killed in 1913, is discussed on pages 84-85.)

Musgrave, Mark E. 1938. "Ben Lilly—Last of the Mountain Men." *American Forests*, Vol. 44, No. 8 (August), pp. 349-351, 379-380.

New Mexico Department of Game and Fish. 1967. *New Mexico Wildlife Management.* New Mexico Department of Game and Fish, Santa Fe.

Pearce, T. M., ed. 1965. *New Mexico Place Names: A Geographical Dictionary.* University of New Mexico Press, Albuquerque.

Peoples, Morgan. 1978. "Ben Lilly's Last Visit to Louisiana, August 11, 1920." *North Louisiana Historical Association Journal*, Vol. 9, pp. 37-41.

Poole, Arthur J., and Viola S. Schantz, compilers. 1942. *Catalog of the Type Specimens of Mammals in the United States National Museum, Including the Biological Survey's Collection.* U.S. National Museum Bulletin No. 178. Smithsonian Institution, Washington, D.C. (Ben Lilly's White Mountains, Arizona, grizzly is listed on page 87.)

Richards, Raymond. 1922. "Veteran Hunter of Big Game Here After 54 Years on Trail." *The Denver Post*, November 5.

Rider, Jim. 1991. "Ben Lilly stays alive in kids." *The Bastrop (La.) Daily Enterprise*, May 24.

_____. 1992. "Relatives tracing family legend." *The Bastrop (La.) Daily Enterprise*, June 15.

_____. 1992. "Letters from Ben Lilly." *The Bastrop (La.) Daily Enterprise*, October 30.

_____. 1992. "A memorial for Lilly, maybe?" *The Bastrop (La.) Daily Enterprise*, November 2.

_____. 1992. "Sketches of a time past." *The Bastrop (La.) Daily Enterprise*, November 4.

_____. 1992. "Interest expressed in Lilly Memorial." *The Bastrop (La.) Daily Enterprise*, November 5.

_____. 1992. "Letters lift spirits of aging Lilly." *The Bastrop (La.) Daily Enterprise*, November 6.

_____. 1992. "Farming was not for Ben Lilly." *The Bastrop (La.) Daily Enterprise*, November 9.

_____. 1992. "Monday morning scatter shooting: For A Memorial." *The Bastrop (La.) Daily Enterprise*, November 23.

Roosevelt, Theodore. 1908. "In the Louisiana Canebrakes." Reprinted in: *American Bears: Selections from the Writings of Theodore Roosevelt*. Edited by Paul Schullery. Colorado Associated University Press, Boulder, 1983, pp. 154-169. (First published in the January 1908 issue of *Scribner's Magazine*.)

_____. 1919. *Theodore Roosevelt's Letters to His Children.* Edited by Joseph B. Bishop. Charles Scribner's Sons, New York. (Roosevelt's October 1907 letter to his daughter Ethel in which he described Ben Lilly is reproduced on pages 209-211.)

Salars, Cal. 1998. "Personal communications with Neil Carmony regarding the Grant County, New Mexico, poor farm." (In the 1930s the county poor farm where Ben Lilly spent his last years was supervised by Mrs. Mary Roberts Hines, Cal Salars' aunt.

Sources and References

As a boy, Cal visited the place often and talked with Ben Lilly on numerous occasions. Mr. Salars was born in 1924 and now lives in Silver City.)

Salmon, M. H. 1991. "Ben Lilly Revisited." In: *Tales of the Chase: Hound Dogs, Catfish, and Other Pursuits Afield.* High-Lonesome Books, Silver City, New Mexico, pp. 42-55.

Schmidt, John L., and Douglas L. Gilbert, eds. 1978. *Big Game of North America: Ecology and Management.* Stackpole Books, Harrisburg, Pennsylvania.

Schullery, Paul, ed. 1983. *American Bears: Selections from the Writings of Theodore Roosevelt.* Colorado Associated University Press, Boulder. (Roosevelt's story about his Louisiana bear hunt with Ben Lilly is reprinted on pages 154-169.)

Schullery, Paul. 1988. *The Bear Hunter's Century: Profiles from the Golden Age of Bear Hunting.* Reprint: High-Lonesome Books, Silver City, New Mexico, 1998. (Includes biographical sketches of Ben Lilly and Holt Collier on pages 185-203 and 205-226.)

_____. 1992. *The Bears of Yellowstone.* Third edition, revised. High Plains Publishing Company, Worland, Wyoming. (Decades of bear research are summarized in this book.)

Shannon, S. C. 1992. *Ghost Dancer—The Legend—Tales of the Southwest—Haunting Stories of the Mountain Men.* Vol. 2. Privately published by the author, Silver City, New Mexico.

_____. 1993. *Ghost Dancer II—The Legend—Tales of the Southwest—Haunting!* A Scribe Ltd. Publication, Carlsbad, New Mexico. (Privately published by the author.)

Shaw, Harley. 1980. "Ecology of the Mountain Lion in Arizona: A final Report." Research Branch, Arizona Game and Fish Department, Phoenix, 14 pp.

_____. 1987. *Mountain Lion Field Guide.* Special Report Number 9. Third edition, revised. Arizona Game and Fish Department, Phoenix.

_____. 1989. *Soul Among Lions: The Cougar as Peaceful Adversary.* Johnson Books, Boulder, Colorado.

Sitton, Thad. 1995. *Backwoodsmen: Stockmen and Hunters along a Big Thicket River Valley.* University of Oklahoma Press, Norman.

Stevens, Montague. 1943. *Meet Mr. Grizzly: A Saga on the Passing of the Grizzly Bear.* Reprint: High-Lonesome Books, Silver City, New Mexico, 1987.

Sweet, John R. 1998. "Western Houndsmen Heritage Project." *Full*

Cry, February, pp. 81-83. (Ninety-year-old Jesse E. Hawley [born in 1907] described his only meeting with Ben Lilly [1926] in this article. See Hawley 1998.)

Tarrant, Bill. 1988. "The Man Who Loved Dogs." *Field and Stream*, February, pp. 56-57, 86-89.

Tinsley, Jim Bob. 1987. *The Puma, Legendary Lion of the Americas*. Texas Western Press, University of Texas at El Paso.

Truett, Joe C., and Daniel W. Lay. 1984. *Land of Bears and Honey: A Natural History of East Texas*. University of Texas Press, Austin.

Turner, Allton. 1968. "As We Remember Ben Lilly: Photos and Story of a Great Wilderness Hunter." *La Ventura Magazine* (Saturday supplement to *The Silver City Daily Press*), December 7.

W. L. P. 1887. "With the Bears in Coon Bayou." *Forest and Stream*, February 10, pp. 46-47.

White, Warren. 1994. "The Story of Ben Lilly." (Address given June 4, 1994, at the Snyder Museum, Bastrop, Louisiana.)

_____. 1997. "Personal communications with Neil Carmony regarding the Ben Lilly memorial in Mer Rouge, Louisiana." (Warren White spearheaded the effort to fund the monument honoring Ben Lilly that was erected in May 1997.)

Winn, Fred. 1923. "Ben Lilly, a Twentieth Century Daniel Boone." *American Forestry*, Vol. 29, No. 355 (July), pp. 398-399.

_____. 1937. "Ben Lilly—Trapper, Mountaineer. *American Cattle Producer*, Vol. 18, No. 9 (February), pp. 13-14.

_____. 1943. "Ben Lilly, Lion Hunter." *The American Mercury*, Vol. 56, No. 233 (May), p. 636. (Letter to the magazine's editor.)

Woolsey, Norman G. 1998. "Personal communications with Neil Carmony regarding Ben Lilly." (Norm Woolsey, who now lives in Mesa, Arizona, met Ben Lilly once circa 1930 at Cliff, New Mexico. Norm (born in 1922) was about eight years old at the time of their meeting.)

Works Projects Administration. 1937. *Idaho: A Guide in Word and Picture*. Federal Writers' Projects of the Works Projects Administration, Vardis Fisher State Director. Caxton Printers, Caldwell, Idaho.

Young, Stanley P., and Edward A. Goldman. 1946. *The Puma, Mysterious American Cat*. Part I (by S. P. Young): "History, Life Habits, Economic Status, and Control." Pp. 1-173. Reprint: Dover Publications, New York, 1964.

INDEX

Alma, NM, 23, 24, 45, 63, 83, 85, 169, 180
Alpine, AZ, 23, 63, 77, 78, 81, 83, 157
American National Livestock Association, 10, 11, 14, 165
Animas, NM, 44
Animas Creek, NM, 15
Animas Foundation, 17
Animas Mountains, NM, 15, 18, 20, 46
Apache National Forest, AZ/NM, 24, 80
Armour, Mr., 25-27
Bailey, Vernon, 194 n. 16
Barber's ranch, NM, 49
Bastrop, LA, 152, 164
Bayard, NM, 10
Bear, black, 3, 4, 7-9, 14-24, 29-32, 65-69, 86-112, 161, 162; protected as game in Arizona and New Mexico, 21, 162; not always black, 15; how to distinguish from grizzly, 68; as killer of cattle, 66-67; specimens collected by Lilly, 190-191
Bear chased through three states, 17-19
Bear, grizzly, 20-23, 28-29, 59-65; killed in Mexico, 7, 118, 191, 199; killed in Arizona, 8, 22-23, 62-63, 162, 167, 188, 189, 191, 199; tracked near Taos, New Mexico, 86, 96, 97, 101; sign seen in Idaho, 96, 97, 101; poisoned in Idaho, 86, 99, 101; "three-state" bear not a grizzly, 18-19; extermination in Southwest and Mexico, 21; size of, 23, 63; how to tell from black bear, 68; specimens collected by Lilly, 191, 199-200
Bear Lake, LA, 4
Bebb, Dr., 165, 167
Ben Lilly Legend, The (book), 2, 11, 33, 143, 145, 146
Big Creek, ID, 103
Big Dry Creek, NM, 45, 46, 155, 182
Big Thicket, TX, 3-4, 115-117, 190-193
Biological Survey, 3, 8, 24, 25, 42, 43, 49, 70, 136, 150, 153-155
Black Canyon, NM, 25, 27
Black Range, NM, 12, 25, 156
Blue (Blue Post Office), AZ, 23, 24, 48, 77, 82, 155, 156, 159, 181, 191
Blue River, AZ, 8, 20, 21, 23-25, 45, 48-50, 62, 63, 70, 71,

75, 81, 82, 84, 85, 131, 154, 157-160, 191
Bobcat, 8, 44, 78, 159; specimens collected by Lilly, 191
Bonne Idee Bayou, LA, 2, 151, 172
Bowe, Fay, 114, 120, 170
Brown, David E., 150
Brownsville, TX, 169, 175, 177, 183
Campbell Blue (creek), AZ, 157
Carter, Elma (niece), 173, 174
Catron County, NM, 85
Chihuahua, Mex., 7, 17-19, 21, 52, 114, 118, 162, 188, 190-191
Chihuahua City, Mex., 7, 19, 118, 154
Chloride, NM, 25, 165, 191
Cliff, NM, 68, 135
Clifton, AZ, 20-23, 45, 70, 73-75, 81, 82, 153, 154, 191
Coahuila, Mex., 7, 19, 52, 161, 190-193
Collier, Holt, 4
Collyge, Billy Joe, 142
Cooley, Hal, 141
Cooper ranch, NM, 79, 80
Cosper, Toles, 45, 74, 82, 154, 157
Coyote, 8, 28, 44, 51, 90, 103, 104, 113, 159; specimens collected by Lilly, 191
Crook (dog), 88-96, 98, 102-104, 108, 110, 126
Culberson, Victor, 10, 28, 31, 42, 171

Dean, Reed, 79
Depp's ranch, NM, 49
Devil Canyon, NM, 78-80
Diamond A Ranch, NM, 17, 18, 45
Diamond Bar Ranch, NM, 25-28, 42
Dillon Mountain, NM, 78, 80, 83
Dobie, J. Frank, 2, 10-13, 33, 59, 87, 143, 145, 146, 150, 169
Dodd, Elmer Cecil (son-in-law), 169-177, 183
Double Circle Ranch, AZ, 154
Drake, J. B., 164-165
Duncan, Leolla Tirey, 181, 182
Dunton, W. Herbert, op. 1, 87
Eagle Creek, AZ, 71, 81, 82, 153, 154, 159
Eagle Pass, TX, 7, 19, 161, 177
East and South Texas, Lilly's hunts in, 3-4, 115-117, 190-193
Eisely, Walter Bartlett ("Bart," son-in-law), 169-177
Elk, 95, 108-110, 168
El Paso, TX: Ben Lilly gives talk at, 10, 14, 165; Ben Lilly has photos taken at, 169, 170; Hugh Lilly moves to, 169, 179
Escudilla Mountain, AZ, 62
Fierro, NM, 161, 165
Fisher, Albert K., 8, 12, 153, 156, 157, 160
Fisher, Robert D., 190, 199-200
Foote Creek, AZ, 48, 50

Index

Forsythe, Harvey, 10, 59
Gallego, Chihuahua, 7, 118, 154, 191
Gila National Forest, NM, 9, 25, 136, 141, 148, 150
Gila River, NM, 25, 68
Gila Wilderness, NM, 25, 26, 150
Glaze, Mr., 28
Goforth, Andrew Jackson, 138
Goforth, Emmett, 138
Goforth, Leslie, 138
Golley, E. H., 49
Goode, Monroe H., 86, 169, 170
G.O.S. Ranch, NM, 9, 10, 27, 28, 42, 134, 135, 141, 161, 162, 165, 168, 171, 177, 181, 186, 188
Grant County, NM, poor farm, 10, 181, 182
Gray, Michael, 17
Gray Ranch, NM, 17
Greenlee County, AZ, 8, 70, 85, 190, 191
Griffin, Ben, 161
Guthrie, John D., 24
Gutierrez, Manuel, 130, 137, 147
Hamberlin, Monroe, 55
Hannagan Meadow, AZ, 23
Hanover, NM, 181, 182
Hansen, Kevin, 31
Hardin County, TX, 3, 190-193
Harp, Tom, 150
Hawley, J. E., 200
Hazlehurst, MS, 171, 181
Hermosa, NM, 25
Hibben, Frank C., 118, 153, 194 n. 18
Hickel, Harry, 150
Hines, Mary Roberts (Mrs. Jess Hines), 182
Hodge, H. L., 42
Hoffmeister, Donald F., 194 n. 18
Hollister, Ned, 3, 153, 155
Hooker, Jack, 89
Hooks, Ben, 3
Hooks, Bud, 3
Horton Creek, AZ, 23, 62, 191
Hotchkiss, Walter W., 136, 137
Housholder, Bob, 194 n. 18
Idaho, Lilly's hunt in, 9, 86-113
Indian Creek, NM, 25
Jaguar, 45, 46, 154-157
James brothers' ranch, NM, 25, 165
Jessen, L. A., 10, 165, 167
Johnson's goat ranch, NM, 25
Jones, Sam, 168
Kemper County, MS, 2
Kiene, L. L., 3, 4
Laney, Mr., 78
Laney's ranch, NM, 79, 82
Lang ranch, NM, 45
Largo Canyon, NM, 79, 80
Lee, Dale, 1, 12
Lee, Ernest, 1
Lewis, Bill, 81
Ligon, J. Stokley, 8, 78, 126, 129, 131, 136, 150, 153-157
Lilly, Ada Mai (daughter, Mrs. Walter B. Eisely), 2, 10, 165, 169-178, 180-184
Lilly, Albert (father), 2
Lilly, Beatrice Verna (daughter,

Ben Lilly's Tales

Mrs. Elmer C. Dodd), 2, 10, 151, 169-178, 180, 183
Lilly, Benjamin Vernon: early life, 2; marriages and children, 2, 3; as museum collector, 3, 190-193; Big Thicket hunt, 3-4, 115-117; hunt with Teddy Roosevelt, 4-7; religious beliefs, 5-6; time in Mexico, 7, 19, 118, 161-162, 190-193; grizzlies killed by, 7, 8, 22-23, 62-63, 118, 191, 199-200; as Biological Survey employee, 8-9, 70-85, 153-160; hunt with W. H. McFadden, 9, 86-113; as hunter for G.O.S. Ranch, 9, 181; as trapper, 17-18, 74, 95-98, 101, 110; talk in El Paso, 10, 14, 165; meeting with Frank Dobie, 10; deafness, 35; use of guide dogs, 35; use of slow track hounds, 44, 62, 163; use of hunting horn, 9, 26, 90, 113, 146; memorials to, 11, 148-152; relations with daughters, 169-170; drawings by, 9, 143-147, 171-174, 176; knives made by, 9, 166, 170-171; taken to poor farm, 10, 181-182; death, 10, 182
Lilly, Hugh (son), 2, 10, 169, 172, 175, 179-180, 183
Lilly, Jennie (sister, Mrs. J. C. Franklin), 171, 178
Lilly, Joe R. (Brother), 9, 166, 169
Lilly, Lelia Bunckley (first wife), 2
Lilly, Margaret ("Maggie," sister, Mrs. E. Hunter Mills), 9, 169, 171, 178
Lilly, Margaret Ann McKay (mother), 2
Lilly, Mary Etta Sisson (second wife), 2, 3, 169, 179-180
Lilly, Sarah Frances ("Sallie," sister, Mrs. James H. Rogers), 171, 173, 174, 178, 181, 182
Lilly, Verna. See Lilly, Beatrice Verna
Lilly, Vernon (uncle), 2
Lilly, Vernon ("Dick," son), 2
Little Blue Creek, AZ, 20, 21
Lomax, Delores, 179, 182
Lost Spring Canyon, NM, 79-81
Louisiana, Lilly's hunts in, 4-7, 190-193
Luna, NM, 23, 78, 82, 83
McFadden, William H., 9, 11, 86-88, 97, 105, 110-113, 171, 176, 181, 185, 186, 189
McIlhenny, John A., 4
McKeefie (?), Barney, 159
McKeefie (?), Pat, 159
McKeen, Hugh, 45, 158
Marland Oil Co., 86
Merriam, C. Hart, 7, 153, 155
Mer Rouge, LA, 2, 11, 114, 120, 125, 148, 150-152, 170, 172, 174, 180
Mer Rouge Lions Club, 11
Metcalfe, Clive, 4

Metcalfe, Harley, 4
Milligan's Mill, AZ, 157
Mills, Margaret (niece), 171
Mimbres, NM, 170, 173, 175-177
Mimbres Valley, NM, 10, 181, 191
Mississippi, 2, 52, 53, 55-57, 150, 167, 171, 181, 187, 188
Mississippi River, 29, 52, 55-57, 161, 163
Mogollon Mountains, NM, 155
Monroe, LA, 170
Morehouse Parish, LA, 2, 164
Mountain lion: modern research regarding, 14, 21-22, 26, 31, 34, 37, 39, 41-42, 48, 71, 84; never attack people in New Mexico, 56, 57; five-toed track seen, 49-50; five kittens in one litter found, 26; specimens collected by Lilly, 191 . See also Panther
Múzquiz, Coahuila, 19, 190-193
National Museum. See U.S. National Museum
National Rifle Association, 163, 164
N.O. Bar Ranch, AZ, 154
Northeast Louisiana University, Monroe, 144
Oak Grove, LA, 164, 165
O'Brien, Tom, 10, 175, 177, 181
Ocelot, 161; specimens collected by Lilly, 191
Otter, 161; specimens collected by Lilly, 192
Pankey's ranch, NM, 25

Panther, 3, 7, 52-58; killed people in the South, 52-58. See also Mountain lion
Parker, John M., 4
Pecos River, NM, 44, 46
Ponca City, OK, 86, 87, 105
Porterfield, Melvin, 150
Producer, The (magazine), 11, 13, 14, 167
Red Mountain, AZ, 45, 46, 73, 155
Reserve, NM, 49, 83, 85, 156, 191
Richards, Raymond, 186
Rider, Jim, 152
Rio Grande, 7, 19, 44, 46, 161
Rogers, James H. (Brother-in-law), 171,178
Roosevelt, Ethel, 4, 5
Roosevelt, Theodore, 4-7, 148, 149, 151, 185, 188
Salars, Cal, 182
Saliz Mountains, NM, 49, 50
Sanborn, Frank, 118
Sanders, Gary, 12
San Francisco Mountains, NM, 82
San Francisco River, AZ/NM, 20, 24, 49, 63, 77, 78, 80, 82, 85, 158
Santa Rita, NM, 10, 59, 166
Sapillo Creek, NM, 135, 138
Shreveport, LA, 9, 169
Sierra County, NM, 191
Sierra del Carmen, Coahuila, 19
Sierra Madre, Mex., 19
Sierra San Luis, Chihuahua/Sonora, 17, 18

Sierra Santa Rosa, Coahuila, 19, 161
Silver City, NM, 9-11, 19, 23, 89, 134, 139, 142, 148, 150, 152, 163, 171, 180-182, 186
Silver City Museum, 129, 131-134, 139, 141, 163
Socorro, NM, 78, 79, 81
Socorro County, NM, 85, 191
Sonora, Mex., 17, 18, 52, 188
Spur Cross Ranch, AZ, 153
Strickrott, John, 4, 115-117
Talmage, Thomas DeWitt, 5
Tallulah, LA, 170, 175-177, 182, 191, 192
Taos, NM, 68, 86, 87, 96, 97, 99, 101
Teague, Scott, 86
Tensas Bayou, LA, 4, 5, 148, 151, 161, 191
Thompson, J. B. ("Jack"), 136
Thompson, Johnny, 136
Tirey, Leolla. See Duncan, Leolla Tirey
Tirey, Margaret, 181
Tirey, Roy, 181
Toriette Lakes, NM, 80
Traps and trapping, 6, 17, 18, 24, 28, 49, 74, 82, 95-98, 101, 110
Turkey, wild, 19, 46, 49, 56, 58, 161, 168, 177
Turner, Beth, 138
U.S. National Museum, 3, 7, 8, 18, 23, 118, 153, 187, 190
University of Texas, Austin, 11, 183
Wall, Lloyd, 150
West Carroll Parish, LA, 53, 161, 192
White Mountains, AZ, 8, 23, 49, 62, 162, 185, 188, 190, 192
White, Warren, 11, 125, 152
Wilcox County, AL, 2
Winn, Fred, 150
Wolf, 18, 24, 27, 28, 44, 47, 51, 105, 157, 158, 160, 161; specimens collected by Lilly, 191
Woolsey, Lars Walter, 135
Woolsey, Norman G., 135
Wyatt, Ken, 151
Y Bar Y Ranch, AZ, 74

ABOUT THE EDITOR

Outdoorsman and amateur naturalist Neil Carmony was born in Tucson, Arizona, in 1941 and has lived there ever since. Over the years he heard and read many tales about Ben Lilly, some factual, some fanciful, all enjoyable. But the full story of Ben's exploits remained untold. This inspired Mr. Carmony to search out Ben Lilly's own writings and prepare them for publication. Neil Carmony is the editor/author of several other books including *Afield With J. Frank Dobie: Tales of Critters, Campfires, and the Hunting Trail* and *Onza! The Hunt for a Legendary Cat*. Both of these works are published by High-Lonesome Books and are must reading for people who treasure superb hunting stories.

HIGH-LONESOME BOOKS

"Published in the Greatest Country Out-of-Doors"

At **HIGH-LONESOME BOOKS** we have a great variety of titles for enthusiasts of the Southwest and the great Outdoors -- new, used, and rare books of the following:

Southwest History

Wilderness Adventure

Natural History

Hunting

Sporting Dogs

Mountain Men

Fishing

Country Living

Environment

Our catalog is FREE for the asking. Write or call.

HIGH-LONESOME BOOKS
P. O. Box 878
Silver City, New Mexico
88062
505-388-3763

Also, come visit our bookshop in the country at High-Lonesome Road near Silver City